YOUTH EDUCATION AND UNEMPLOYMENT PROBLEMS

AN INTERNATIONAL PERSPECTIVE

Margaret S. Gordon

with a chapter by

Martin Trow

D1245842

CARNEGIE COUNCIL ON POLICY STUDIES
IN HIGHER EDUCATION

YOUTH EDUCATION AND UNEMPLOYMENT PROBLEMS

An International Perspective
       by Margaret S. Gordon
          with a chapter by Martin Trow

The Carnegie Council on Policy Studies in Higher Education, 2150 Shattuck Avenue, Berkeley, California 94704, has sponsored publication of this report as part of a continuing effort to obtain and present significant information for public discussion. The views expressed are those of the authors.

Library of Congress Catalog Card Number LC 79-54989

International Standard Book Number ISBN 0-931050-14-6

Manufactured in the United States of America

Education and Youth Employment
in Contemporary Societies

A Series of Special Studies

BELGIUM
Henri Janne

GREAT BRITAIN
Stuart Maclure

JAPAN
Hidetoshi Kato

MEXICO AND SOUTH ASIA
*Alberto Hernández Medina, Carlos
Muñoz Izquierdo/Manzoor Ahmed*

POLAND
Barbara Liberska

SWEDEN AND DENMARK
Gösta Rehn, K. Helveg Petersen

FEDERAL REPUBLIC OF GERMANY
Klaus von Dohnanyi

AN INTERNATIONAL PERSPECTIVE
Margaret S. Gordon
with a chapter by
Martin Trow

These publications are available from the Carnegie Council on Policy Studies in Higher Education, 2150 Shattuck Avenue, Berkeley, California 94704.

The Carnegie Council Series

The following publications are available from Jossey–Bass Inc., Publishers, 433 California Street, San Francisco, California 94104.

The Federal Role in Postsecondary Education: Unfinished Business, 1975-1980
The Carnegie Council on Policy Studies in Higher Education

More Than Survival: Prospects for Higher Education in a Period of Uncertainty
The Carnegie Foundation for the Advancement of Teaching

Making Affirmative Action Work in Higher Education: An Analysis of Institutional and Federal Policies with Recommendations
The Carnegie Council on Policy Studies in Higher Education

Presidents Confront Reality: From Edifice Complex to University Without Walls
Lyman A. Glenny, John R. Shea, Janet H. Ruyle, Kathryn H. Freschi

Progress and Problems in Medical and Dental Education: Federal Support Versus Federal Control
The Carnegie Council on Policy Studies in Higher Education

Low or No Tuition: The Feasibility of a National Policy for the First Two Years of College
The Carnegie Council on Policy Studies in Higher Education

Managing Multicampus Systems: Effective Administration in an Unsteady State
Eugene C. Lee, Frank M. Bowen

Challenges Past, Challenges Present: An Analysis of American Higher Education Since 1930
David D. Henry

The States and Higher Education: A Proud Past and a Vital Future
The Carnegie Foundation for the Advancement of Teaching

Educational Leaves for Employees: European Experience for American Consideration
Konrad von Moltke, Norbert Schneevoigt

Faculty Bargaining in Public
Higher Education: A Report and
Two Essays
*The Carnegie Council on Policy
Studies in Higher Education,
Joseph W. Garbarino, David E.
Feller, Matthew W. Finkin*

Investment in Learning: The
Individual and Social Value of
American Higher Education
*Howard R. Bowen
with the collaboration of Peter
Clecak, Jacqueline Powers Doud,
Gordon K. Douglass*

Missions for the College Curriculum:
A Contemporary Review with Sug-
gestions
*The Carnegie Foundation for the
Advancement of Teaching*

Handbook on Undergraduate
Curriculum
Arthur Levine

Curriculum: A History of
the American Undergraduate
Course of Study Since 1636
Frederick Rudolph

Selective Admissions in Higher
Education: Comment and
Recommendations and Two Reports
*The Carnegie Council on Policy
Studies in Higher Education,
Winton H. Manning, Warren W.
Willingham, Hunter M. Breland,
and Associates*

The States and Private
Higher Education: Problems
and Policies in a New Era
*The Carnegie Council on Policy
Studies in Higher Education*

Fair Practices in Higher Education:
Rights and Responsibilities of
Students and Their Colleges in a
Period of Intensified Competition
for Enrollments
*The Carnegie Council on Policy
Studies in Higher Education*

Next Steps for the 1980s
in Student Financial Aid:
A Fourth Alternative
*The Carnegie Council on Policy
Studies in Higher Education*

*The following technical reports are available from the Carnegie
Council on Policy Studies in Higher Education, 2150 Shattuck Avenue,
Berkeley, California 94704.*

The States and Higher Education:
A Proud Past and a Vital Future
SUPPLEMENT to a Commentary of
The Carnegie Foundation for the
Advancement of Teaching
*The Carnegie Foundation for the
Advancement of Teaching*

Changing Practices in
Undergraduate Education
*Robert Blackburn, Ellen
Armstrong, Clifton Conrad,
James Didham, Thomas McKune*

Contents

Foreword

Several years ago, as part of a program to study the transition made by young people from school to work in modern industrial societies, the Carnegie Council decided to sponsor a group of essays on the situation of youth in contemporary societies. Each essay was to focus on an individual country and to be written by an expert on youth in that country. Rising youth unemployment was of growing concern in nearly all of the industrial democracies, and debate was also increasing about whether educational systems were adequately preparing young people for a productive life in a society of advanced technology. Thus, our plans called for essays that would be concerned not only with growing efforts to combat youth unemployment through manpower policies but also with educational issues. In this respect, these essays differ from much that is written about the youth problem, for most publications address either labor market issues or educational questions. Rarely are the two topics considered as part of the central problem of the transition from school to work in the last quarter of the twentieth century. We shall also consider both manpower and educational policies in a forthcoming report on youth in the United States.

Originally we planned to confine these essays to industrialized nations—predominantly industrial democracies—as well as Poland (to shed light on the transition from school to work in an Eastern European socialist country). However, when the opportunity arose to include two essays on less developed countries, one on Mexico and one on four countries of South Asia, we welcomed the chance to gain insights into similarities and differences between the problems of youth in developing countries and in the advanced industrial nations.

When the essays were completed, their combined length was so formidable that we published a separate volume on each country. These volumes began to appear as publications of the Carnegie Council early in 1979.

The present volume includes Margaret Gordon's comparative analysis of the causes of youth unemployment in Western industrial countries. It also includes a summary and commentary on each of the country studies by Margaret Gordon and Martin Trow's "Reflections on Youth Problems and Policies in United States," which considers the American youth problem in light of the experience of other countries.

Margaret Gordon's essay is concerned with the causes of youth unemployment in Western industrialized countries that are suggested by the usual sources of labor market data. She concludes that youth unemployment is not primarily a cyclical problem, nor is it chiefly the result of the bulge in the youth population of industrial countries in the 1960s due to the "baby boom" that followed World War II. Rather, the youth unemployment problem that has affected all Western industrialized countries in the late 1970s is largely the result of structural changes on the demand side of the labor market that have reduced employment opportunities for young people compared with those for adults. She also includes a useful summary of the manpower and educational policies in other countries that she considers of value to American policy makers.

Martin Trow's essay emphasizes aspects of the youth unemployment problem in the United States that are less relevant in Western Europe or that receive little emphasis in the European essays, especially (1) the secondary labor market, which is an important source of jobs for young people in the United States, but which is more likely to provide jobs for foreign workers in Western Europe; (2) illicit employment—or the underground labor market—which plays an important role in the American inner city but is scarcely mentioned in the European essays; and (3) the importance of distinguishing among groups of youth—

the advantaged, the disadvantaged, the alienated, and the deprived—for whom very different policies are needed. Trow suggests, in particular, that existing manpower policies in the United States are not reaching the deprived, who are most desperately in need of services.

Some of the themes developed in the essays on other countries that are summarized in this volume are of particular interest for their relevance to policy makers in the United States and elsewhere:

1. Stuart Maclure's illuminating discussion of the potential effects of Britain's uniform guarantee of £18 a week to the sizable proportion of unemployed youth in Britain that is enrolled in manpower programs. Such earnings may induce these young people away from school, for which weekly support stipends are much lower and are limited to relatively few low-income students in secondary schools. This raises a question about American manpower programs for youth, since no significant income support program exists for high school students except for families on welfare.

2. Gösta Rehn's account of the experiment in developing expanded youth employment services in several large Swedish cities, indicating considerable success in developing jobs in the private sector for young people, but showing that many of these jobs were temporary and low paid, such as those in the secondary labor market described by dual labor market theorists in the United States. The Swedish experiment also yielded valuable data on the characteristics of youthful jobseekers, some of whom were particularly hard to place and resembled the "deprived" youth described by Martin Trow.

3. Kato's description of education and training programs conducted by large employers in Japan, in which people of high school age receive the equivalent of a high school education combined with intensive occupational training under company sponsorship and at company expense.

4. Barbara Liberska's discussion of the mismatch between the types of jobs obtained by educated young workers in Poland and the types of jobs to which they aspire, suggesting that, even

where manpower requirements are an important criterion in educational planning, as they are in Eastern Europe, perfect adjustments between manpower demand and supply are difficult to achieve.

5. Petersen's description of residential centers for unemployed young people in Denmark, which are located in farmlike surroundings that not only offer a combination of work experience and education but are actually run to a large extent by the young people.

I also find much that is relevant to American problems in the descriptions of educational issues in other countries, particularly at the secondary level. Rising youth unemployment has heightened debate in Western Europe about educational issues, in large part because in country after country it has been found that the least educated young people, and especially those who have dropped out of school, are the most likely to be unemployed. But concern over the relationship between secondary education and employment actually started earlier and was increasingly evident in the first half of the 1970s. The prolongation of compulsory education, as well as the rising proportion of young people going on to postcompulsory education, which occurred throughout Europe in the 1960s, had uncovered the fact that by no means all young people benefited from continuing their education beyond age 14 or 15. Those who were academically inclined and preparing for higher education usually encountered no difficulties, but prolonged education was ill suited to many young people (especially those from families at the lower rungs of the socioeconomic ladder) who continued in school largely because of either legal compulsion or parental pressure and were learning very little. With our earlier thrust toward mass education at the high school level, this problem developed much earlier in the United States.

Henri Janne's presentation of the data on "laggers" in the Belgian schools is particularly enlightening in this respect, because it shows that, even in a country largely without racial differences, the problem of children who fall behind in school is serious and highly influenced by the socioeconomic status of the parents.

As a result of the recognition of this problem, most countries of Western Europe now offer almost no support for any additional prolonging of compulsory education. Much of the debate focuses on the appropriate mix of vocational and general education, the desirability of giving students an opportunity to try out several types of vocational programs before choosing one (as in North Rhine–Westphalia), and giving students an opportunity for actual work experience in, say, the last year of compulsory education or even earlier (as in Sweden) before deciding whether to continue in school and what educational "stream" to choose. It is true that in the Federal Republic of Germany, as von Dohnanyi points out, the unions and the Social Democratic party favor a tenth compulsory school year, but this would simply bring the country into line with many other Western European countries.

Perhaps even more relevant to the American scene is the evidence of boredom and dissatisfaction with school. Henri Janne presents results of a survey of 16- to 18-year-olds in Belgium, which show decidedly negative attitudes toward school; interestingly, dissatisfaction was strongest in the highest social classes and weakest in the lowest ones. Such dissatisfaction is not confined to Belgium. At a recent meeting of the Carnegie Council, Torsten Husen, one of the world's leading experts on comparative education and an invited guest at our meeting, indicated that in surveys conducted in a number of different countries a large percentage of youth aged 14 to 16 said that they "hated" school.

Boredom and lack of stimulation in school has long been emphasized by critics of American education, particularly at the high school level. Many of these critics point out that secondary education is the neglected segment of American education, so far as public policy is concerned. Although we have had programs to enrich early childhood education and rapidly increasing student aid to improve access to higher education, we have done next to nothing as a nation to attack the serious problems of our high schools, especially in inner–city areas. This question will receive considerable attention in the Carnegie Council's forthcoming report on youth in the United States.

Interest in exposing young people to a combination of work experience and education at an earlier age in order to combat boredom with school and to give youngsters a greater appreciation of the relevance of school to jobs has been growing in industrial countries and is very much in line with the approach of the proponents of "career education" in the United States. Henri Janne's proposals go even farther than most in this direction. However, it is also fascinating to discover that Manzoor Ahmed views this approach as the way to reform primary schooling in South Asia. The problem there is not just failure of the traditional type of primary school to stimulate the children but the fact that poverty accounts for high drop-out rates from primary schools. Programs in which youngsters could alternate between work and school would make it economically more feasible for them to stay in school and at the same time give more relevance to what they would be learning. As Medina and Izquierdo point out, Mexico has recently emphasized the development of subprofessional schools for youngsters who have completed basic secondary school.

Finally, evidence indicates that the youth unemployment problems of Western Europe may eventually become more like those in the United States. The problems of young Jamaicans in England, of Algerians in France, and of the children of *Gastarbeiter* (guest workers) in various countries are likely to become more serious, as several of our authors suggest. Or, to quote Torsten Husèn, "a new under–class is emerging in Europe composed of those who are neglected in one way or another and have given up."

The German Marshall Fund generously provided support for two international conferences on education and youth employment, which were attended by several of the authors of studies for this project and which have contributed significantly to the Council's deliberations on this subject. The International Council for Educational Development, under the direction of James A. Perkins, helped to coordinate these conferences and also arranged for the participation of the essayists on individual countries in this project. We acknowledge this contribution with profound thanks.

We also wish to extend our thanks to Diana Lorentz for her editorial contributions and to Sylvia Zuck for coordinating manuscript preparation.

CLARK KERR
Chairman,
Carnegie Council on Policy Studies
in Higher Education

1

Youth Unemployment in Western Industrial Countries

Youth unemployment, a problem of serious dimensions in the United States since at least the early 1960s, has recently spread to most other Western industrial countries, prompting pronounced concern and numerous policies to alleviate the problem. The potential social consequences of high youth unemployment may be as important as the economic aspects in stirring national governments to action. As an article in the *New York Times* pointed out, "In American cities rising youth unemployment has been associated with increased crime and other violence, suicides, drug addiction, prostitution. An investigation has found fears running deep in many Common Market countries that they may be headed down a similar path" (Farnsworth, 1976).

In fact, it is doubtful that a direct, causal relationship exists between rising youth unemployment rates and rising juvenile delinquency rates. Although adult crime rates do tend to fluctuate with unemployment rates, no such clear–cut relationship has been established for juvenile delinquency rates (Barton, 1976). However, since juvenile crime rates tend to be higher than crime rates of adults, a rise in the percentage of youth in the total population, which has been experienced by all Western countries at some time in the postwar period, is likely to result in an increase in crime rates.

Policy measures in industrial countries range from emphasizing vocational training to subsidizing private employers who hire youth and creating public service jobs for young people. However, activity is not confined to the labor market. Educational systems, particularly at the secondary level, are being re-examined, with special reference to seeking the appropriate mix between academic and vocational training.

What is the outlook for this problem? Is it a short-term phenomenon that will soon go away or a long-term problem that will be plaguing Western societies for years to come? This is the central question addressed here. At least three possible hypotheses must be considered:

1. The problem is primarily cyclical—especially in Western Europe—and will disappear as economies recover.

2. The problem, resulting primarily from long-term structural changes in the labor market that are associated with advanced industrialization, is likely to persist for the foreseeable future.

3. The problem arises largely on the supply side of the labor market, resulting from the high birth rates in the years after World War II that led to the bulge in the number of teenagers entering the labor market in the 1960s and 1970s. As these baby boom youth are followed by youth born in periods of declining birth rates, youth unemployment differentials will decline.

Two other possible hypotheses could be explored: (1) that the welfare state makes it possible for young people to subsist on the basis of casual or intermittent employment, interspersed with periods of dependence on unemployment insurance or public assistance; and (2) that young people are "choosy" about jobs, refusing to accept those that pay too little or that involve unpleasant working conditions. I have, however, chosen not to include a discussion of either of these two possible explanations of youth unemployment, because I believe that most of the evidence supporting them is anecdotal and that no "hard" evidence exists to indicate that they account for an important part of youth unemployment. Several of the authors of the essays summarized later in this volume—Maclure on Britain, Rehn on Sweden, and von Dohnanyi on West Germany—indicate that they do not believe these factors play an important role in explaining youth unemployment in their countries. Moreover, it is important to recognize that unemployment insurance systems generally require a worker to have been employed a certain minimum number of weeks (e.g., 14 to 20 weeks under state laws in the United States and 26 in Great Britain) in the preceding year to qualify for unemployment benefits. A young person who has been employed only casually or intermittently usually cannot meet this requirement. Evidence does exist, however, as Trow's essay in this volume indicates, that illicit earnings play a role in providing subsistence for at least some unemployed ghetto youth in the United States.

Returning to the three hypotheses to be seriously considered, I would be presumptuous to pretend that I might arrive at a clear-cut answer. The problem is much too new in most countries for one to have any historical perspective, and, even in the United States and Canada, where it is not so new, experts disagree about the outlook. I shall attempt to examine the relevant data, with a view to sorting out demand and supply factors involved and evaluating the three hypotheses above. This attempt is made in the face of the severe inadequacies and incomparabilities of statistics that hamper international comparisons of labor force phenomena.

The General Dimensions of the Problem

In the United States, the unemployment rate has been considerably higher for youth aged 16 to 19 throughout the postwar period than for youth in their early twenties, and thus the teen-age problem arouses the most concern (Figure 1.1). In the early postwar years, the teen-age rate was roughly three times the adult rate, but in the 1960s the differential rose sharply and reached five times the adult rate by the end of the decade. Then, as the adult rate moved upward in the 1970s, the teen-age differential—but not the teen-age rate—moved down. Over the

Figure 1.1. Percentage of civilian labor force unemployed, rate for
adults aged 25 to 54 and rates for youthful age groups, United
States, annual average, 1947 to 1976, and December 1977
(seasonally adjusted), and population growth in youthful
age groups, actual, 1948 to 1976, and projected,
1977 to 1990

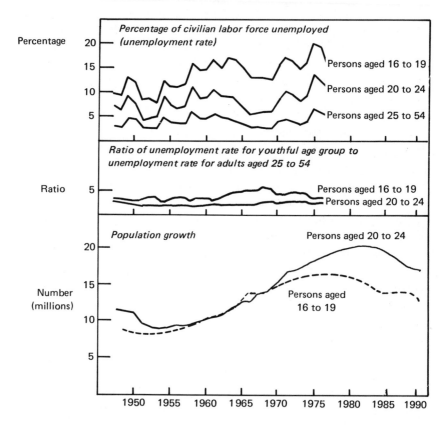

Source: The President (1977); and U.S. Bureau of the Census (1965, 1974, 1976, 1977a and 1977b).

postwar period as a whole, the teen-age unemployment rate has
tended to rise. The differential for those aged 20 to 24 has remained relatively constant, although their unemployment rate
has shown a moderate upward trend.

Teen-age unemployment in the United States is not a cy-clical phenomenon. In fact, the teen-age differential tends to fluctuate in a countercyclical manner—in recessions, layoffs cause adult unemployment rates to rise more sharply than teen-age rates, but adult rates fall more rapidly in economic up-swings. In addition, teen-agers are more likely than adult males to enter the labor force during upswings and to withdraw dur-ing downswings, thus reducing cyclical variations in their unem-ployment rate.

Moreover, the sharp rise in the teen-age unemployment differential in the 1960s coincided with a pronounced rise in the teen-age population and teen-age labor force. This lends some support to the hypothesis that the problem largely stems from the supply side of the labor market and is thus likely to become less serious as the teen-age population declines in the late 1970s and the 1980s (as a result of the decline in the birth rate that became pronounced from the early 1960s on). On the other hand, the 20-to-24 age group is growing rapidly and ex-periencing a rising unemployment trend at present, but the group will begin to decline in size around 1982 or 1983.

Other Western countries, principally those that have expe-rienced an especially sharp rise in the unemployment rate in the last few years, have also encountered a serious problem of youth unemployment (see Figures 1.2 to 1.5). In Italy, however, the overall unemployment rate has not risen appreciably, but recent-ly youth differentials and the absolute number of youthful un-employed have been rising substantially. Perhaps the most dra-matic reason for the consternation over youth unemployment is evidenced in Figure 1.5, which shows enormous increases in the numbers of unemployed youth in the eight countries included.

Another point worth emphasizing is the fact that youth unemployment differentials tend to vary widely despite similar changes over time. Of the countries for which comparable data have been developed (those in Figure 1.4), the highest differen-tial exists in Italy, where persons seeking their first jobs form a large percentage of the unemployed; the lowest differential ex-ists in Japan. These differences, as I found in an earlier study,

Figure 1.2. Unemployment rates, adjusted to international concepts,
selected countries, annual averages 1960 to 1974,
quarterly averages 1975 through third quarter 1978
(seasonally adjusted)

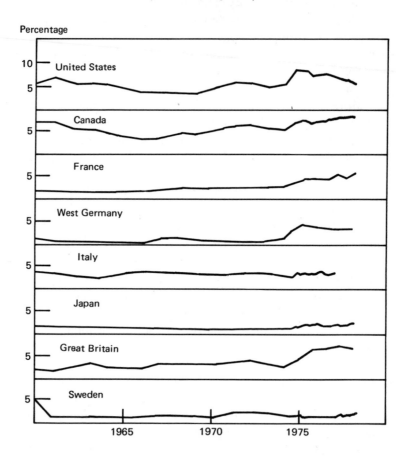

Source: Data for 1960 through the third quarter of 1977 are from U.S. Bureau of Labor Statistics (1978, pp. 19, 21); data for the United States for the next four quarters are from The President (1979, p. 215); data for other countries for the next four quarters are from Organization for Economic Cooperation and Development (1978, p. 13). The adjustments made by the U.S. Bureau of Labor Statistics and OECD differ slightly in some cases. Since the differences are appreciable in the case of Italy, Italian data for the most recent four quarters have been omitted.

**Figure 1.3. Unemployment rates for youthful age groups, adjusted
to United States concepts, selected countries,
selected years, 1968 to 1976**

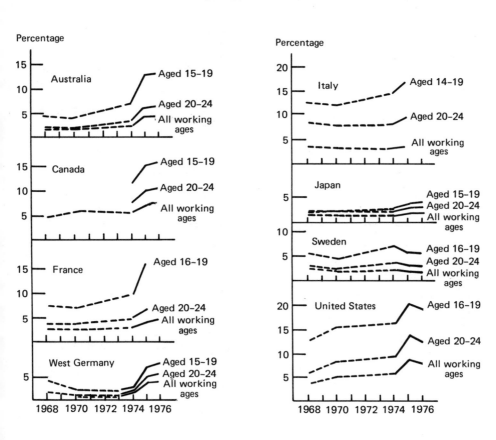

Source: U.S. Bureau of Labor Statistics (1978, pp. 35–36).

seem to be related, among other things, to differences in the
traditional patterns of preparing youth for the labor market
(Gordon, 1965). Until very recently, for example, West Germany
had almost no youth unemployment, except on a small scale in
recessions, because the great majority of school leavers entered
apprenticeships, which provided relatively stable employment.

**Figure 1.4. Ratios of unemployment rates for youthful age groups
to rates for adults aged 25 to 54, adjusted to United States
concepts, selected countries, selected years, 1968 to 1976**

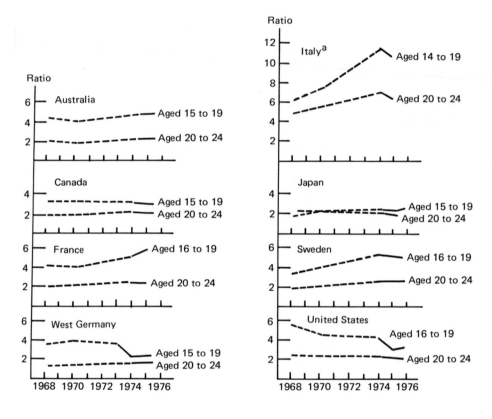

[a]Not adjusted to U.S. concepts.

Source: U.S. Bureau of Labor Statistics (1978, p. 35–36).

The Cyclical Hypothesis

In the United States, as stated above, youth unemployment becomes more serious in recessions, but the phenomenon is not cyclical in the sense that it disappears in periods of prosperity; in fact, the youth unemployment differential tends to behave countercyclically. Although the problem is likely to become less

Figure 1.5. Number of unemployed aged 24 and younger, selected countries, 1967 to 1976

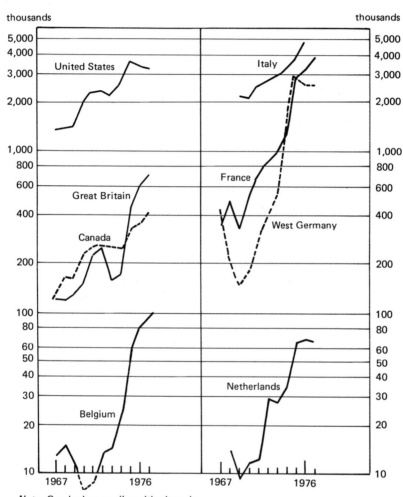

Note: Graphed on semilogarithmic scale.

Source: Commission of the European Communities (1976).

serious in the 1980s, when the size of the youthful population declines, it is unlikely to disappear. We shall come back to this point later.

Because comparable data for most other Western industrial countries have been available only since about 1968, it is much more difficult to determine whether the current youth unemployment problem is largely a result of the recession that began in 1973-74 (and that has left a residue of stubbornly high unemployment rates) or whether it is a longer-term problem. In the early stages of the recession, most of these countries tended to regard rising youth unemployment as a phenomenon that would disappear when national unemployment rates fell. As time has gone on, however, certain long-term trends in the labor market have become apparent that have been adversely affecting youth employment and training opportunities for some time. A number of the country studies prepared for the Carnegie Council on Higher Education (1979) reflect an appreciation of these longer-term trends and a tendency to regard youth unemployment as a problem that will persist for some years.

That youth unemployment is a relatively long-term problem also is the conclusion reached in a report of the Organization for Economic Cooperation and Development (OECD), prepared for its High Level Conference on Youth Unemployment in December 1977:

> The current outlook suggests that aggregate full employment will not be reached in most countries before 1982 under the most optimistic forecasts. Given strong demographic pressures up to 1985 for the [OECD] area as a whole, this implies that the youth labour market will continue to be characterised by excess supply for some years into the future. Thus, failing new major policy initiatives, youth unemployment would continue at excessive levels for at least eight to ten years. . . .
>
> A problem with at least a ten year time perspective can in no way be called "transitory." It could, in fact, imply a generation of lost labour along with the disruptive social and political consequences that may be implied [Organization for Economic Cooperation and Development, 1977c, pp. iv, 28].

Clearly, however, the OECD report suggests that it is because of pressures on the supply side that a youth unemployment problem will persist even after aggregate full employment is reached.

The Demand Hypothesis

It is widely recognized that advancing industrialization imposes certain long-run structural changes in the labor market that impair employment opportunities of young people.

The Decline of Self-Employment

The shift out of agriculture and the sluggishness of nonagricultural self-employment (small business) have greatly reduced family employment opportunities for youth. In fact, the decline in agricultural employment has been going on for decades. True, family employment opportunities in agriculture and small business did not always provide steady employment for young people, but these opportunities did tend to give them work experience, to provide pocket money, and to keep young people from seeking other employment.

The Changing Skill Structure

The decline in the relative importance of unskilled jobs (in which many young people tend to find their first employment) in the course of industrialization has been a major factor on the demand side of the labor market. The rapidly growing trade and service sector does have many unskilled jobs that tend to replace diminishing unskilled openings in the secondary sector (manufacturing, construction, and utilities), but the industries in this sector are also affected to some extent by technological changes that reduce demand for the unskilled. Moreover, many unskilled jobs in this sector are part-time—an advantage to many married women and to students seeking employment, but a disadvantage to nonstudents entering the labor market. In addition, these jobs are often casual or intermittent and tend to lack promotional opportunities.

Technological developments have also altered the skill structure in many manufacturing industries. Mass production methods tend to increase the proportion of semiskilled workers

in relation to both laborers and skilled workers. This development came much earlier in the United States than in Europe,
where mass production methods have been encouraged more
recently by the lowering of trade barriers within the Common
Market. Also important is the rise in the ratio of nonproduction
workers (often engineers) to production workers in technolog-
ically advanced industries, which has occurred particularly in
the U.S. aerospace industries—ordnance, electrical equipment,
aircraft, and instruments—where the proportion of nonproduction workers increased from 23 percent of all workers in 1950
to 38 percent by 1976 (The President, 1977, table C-4). But the
development has gone much farther in states that are heavily
involved in the production of complex equipment for the de-
fense and space programs. In California, for example, well over
50 percent of workers in the aerospace industries were nonproduction workers by the early 1960s. Such developments have
altered training needs, but even more important, declining employment in manufacturing has created few openings for young
beginners.

Growing Rigidities in the Labor Market

In the early decades of the present century, labor–management
relations were far less formalized than they are today. Young
people entered the labor force in unskilled jobs at low pay, often on a part–time or temporary basis. Although this pattern
still exists, far more labor market rules and regulations now bar
young people from certain types of jobs. For example, protec-
tive labor legislation restricts the hours of work for young people, prohibits the employment of minors in proximity to moving
machinery, and requires work permits for employees under a
certain age. Formal seniority provisions in collective bargaining
agreements prevent the employer from laying off older workers
in recessions, which typically results in greater instability of employment for young people, who have little seniority and are
the first to be laid off. Even more restrictive are the legislative
provisions in such countries as Britain, Sweden, and West Germany, which protect adult workers from layoffs. Although these
policies are understandable, they inhibit job opportunities for
youth.

The Costs of Employing Young People

Because of the inexperience and frequent lack of relevant training of young people entering the labor market, employers cannot afford to hire them at wages comparable to those paid adult employees. In many European countries, collective bargaining agreements—and sometimes legislation—establish wage rates that are low for young people but that gradually rise until the age of 20 or 21. But wages of young people relative to those of adults have been rising in the United Kingdom and Sweden, while compensation for apprentices has increased sharply in West Germany. Moreover, throughout the Western world, the rapid growth of fringe benefit expenditures has greatly added to the costs of hiring the young.

In the United States, proposals to provide a reduced minimum wage, or subminimum wage, for youth have generated controversy. (In fact, the Fair Labor Standards Act permits employers to apply for permission to pay lower rates to young people under certain circumstances, but the provision has been little used.) Strongly opposed by organized labor, such proposals have been defeated in Congress on several occasions in recent years. How much a subminimum wage would actually increase employment of young people is not very clear. Studies of the impact of the minimum wage have suggested that it does impair employment opportunities of youth somewhat, but much depends on the ratio of the minimum wage to average earnings (the ratio tends to rise immediately after an increase in the minimum wage but to decline thereafter until the legislation is amended once more). According to one study (Gramlich, 1976), the relative wages of teen-agers would have to drop substantially to increase their employment appreciably (in other words, in the economist's jargon, the wage elasticity of the demand for teen-age labor is low).

Because of the increasing recognition of the high costs of employing youth in relation to their productivity, a number of countries have experimented with various ways of subsidizing employers to hire young people, including direct wage subsidies and exemptions from social security contributions. I shall consider these policies in a discussion of policies to combat youth unemployment.

The Reduced Demand for Apprentices

In a number of European countries in which apprenticeship has played a far more important role in training youth than in the United States, the demand for apprentices has declined appreciably in recent years (Organization for Economic Cooperation and Development, 1978). This has had a significant effect on youth unemployment, because apprenticeships tend to provide stable employment during those critical years when school leavers who do not go into apprenticeships are "shopping around" for acceptable jobs.

The total number of apprentices in West Germany declined slightly from 1967 to 1976, although the decline was apparently reversed in 1977. The declining trend represented a significant change in a country where the great majority of the boys leaving compulsory schooling and a very high percentage of the girls have traditionally gone into apprenticeships. The total number of apprentices also declined appreciably in France over approximately the same period (Organization for Economic Cooperation and Development, 1977a, p. 29), while the number of school leavers entering apprenticeships in Great Britain leveled off between 1965 and 1974.

The West German government has recently taken steps to increase the number of apprentices, as have governments in other countries, but the prospects for decisively reversing the decline in apprenticeships do not appear very promising. Part of the decline may simply reflect the increase in the proportion of young people going on to upper secondary school. This is by no means the whole story in West Germany, as indicated by a growing gap between the supply of apprenticeships and the demand for them. Undoubtedly, technological change has played a role in reducing the demand for apprentices in industries shifting to advanced technology, and it has also led employers to seek young recruits with at least some upper secondary schooling for apprenticeships and other trainee positions. In fact, some disappointed university aspirants in West Germany are now entering apprenticeships. Another factor in the decline in the supply of apprenticeships in West Germany, as already suggested, has been a sharp increase in the compensation of apprenticeships, along with various increases in standards—recently relaxed—which had the effect of increasing the cost of apprenticeship programs to employers.

Locational Factors

In the United States, the geographical decentralization of industry on the demand side, along with increasing concentration of minority-group populations in inner cities on the supply side, has undoubtedly contributed to the exceedingly high unemployment rates among minority-group youth. Similar trends have probably affected certain other countries, such as Great Britain, but they have chiefly played a role where particular population groups are concentrated in slum areas of large cities. Every industrial country also has depressed regions. A number of other countries, as we shall see, have moved more vigorously than has the United States to overcome geographical mismatches between the demand and supply of labor by providing moving allowances to workers.

In an analysis of the experiences of disadvantaged young people seeking employment, the Vocational Foundation, Inc.— a New York City agency specializing in counseling and placement services for young people with correctional backgrounds— produced a list of the problems encountered, some of which we have been discussing.

1. Widespread use of the high school diploma—which these young people do not have—as a "passport to the job market."

2. Use of written tests for job qualification that closely resemble schoolroom exams—with which they cannot cope.

3. Child labor laws and workmen's compensation rules that bar these young people from night shifts, from working where liquor is sold, from using heavy machine tools, construction equipment, forklifts, and other tools common in today's work place.

4. Worksite insurance rates, associated with the workmen's compensation system, that are prohibitively high for employers who might hire these young people and that often raise the cost of employing them to a level substantially above the minimum wage.

5. Arbitrary age limits pertaining to driver's licenses and other licenses that exclude most of them from a wide range of jobs, from beautician to taxi driver.

6. Arrest records and correctional histories that bar them from employment, together with polygraph tests based on these data.

7. Age and education requirements that exclude them from apprenticeships.

8. Minimum wage laws that price them out of the job market.

9. Regulations relating to welfare, food stamps, Medicaid, housing allowances, and legal assistance programs that tie benefits to joblessness and discourage them from working.

10. Just plain race and age discrimination (Vocational Foundation, Inc., n.d.).

Relatively high insurance rates in the United States for vehicles that are to be driven by persons under the age of 25 (particularly young men, whose accident rates tend to be high) should also be mentioned.

A large proportion of jobs in which Vocational Foundation, Inc., has been able to place disadvantaged youth have been relatively low level, part-time, and often temporary jobs, and the organization has found it important to encourage youth to return for additional counseling and placement efforts when jobs terminate or when conflicts between the young person and the employer develop. Another New York City organization, Jobs for Youth, has had a similar experience.

The experience of these organizations tends to confirm the dual labor market theory, developed in an 18-month evaluation study of the Concentrated Employment Program in Boston, part of a national program for placement of the disadvantaged financed by the U.S. Manpower Administration in the late 1960s. The researchers suggested a model of the urban labor market that divides jobs into two categories—primary and secondary. The theory is not entirely new—having been anticipated by earlier theories of labor market segmentation—but it is distinctive in its particular applicability to job opportunities for the disadvantaged. Ghetto workers tend to be confined largely to secondary jobs, which are characterized by one or more of the following: low wages and few fringe benefits, debilitating production speeds, low status, unpleasant working conditions, unsympathetic supervision, inequitable industrial relations arrangements, few promotion opportunities, and unstable employment (U.S. Manpower Administration, 1972, p. 9). Several of these researchers also suggested that "hustling" represented a significant source of alternative income for ghetto workers. (See also Doeringer and Piore, 1971.)

In addition, employer surveys indicate that many employers are reluctant to hire teen-agers. One American study, for example, indicated that a majority of employers in eight cities would not hire persons under 20 for full-time jobs (Gavett and others, 1970). Another study indicated that employers rarely cited high wages as a reason for not hiring youth, mentioning instead such factors as "complicated safety regulations" and uncertainty about youth turnover (National Committee on Employment of Youth, 1975).

The Supply Hypothesis

That a rising youth unemployment problem is primarily attributable to a bulge in the teen-age population seems plausible in view of the fact that most Western industrial countries—and a number of Eastern countries, as well—experienced high birth rates following World War II. However, there were important differences, as Figure 1.6 indicates. The birth rate remained high in the United States and Canada until the latter part of the 1950s, resulting in a bulge in the population aged 16 to 19 that lasted from the early 1960s to the mid-1970s. In some Western European countries, on the other hand, a decline in the birth rate occurred after 1945. Thus the bulge in the population aged 16 to 19 occurred in the early 1960s. In West Germany, Sweden, the United Kingdom, and Japan, the birth rate rose again either in the mid-1950s or in the 1960s, suggesting a large increase in the supply of teen-agers coming onto the labor market from the early 1970s to the early 1980s.

Figure 1.6. Crude birth rates, selected countries, 1940 to 1974

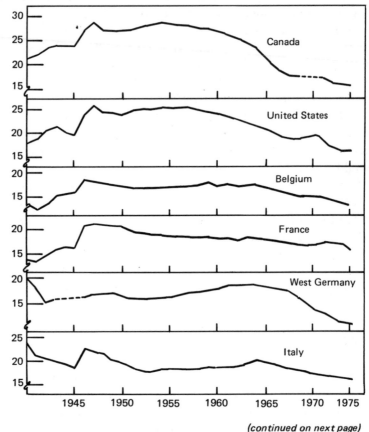

(continued on next page)

In contrast with the situation in the United States and Canada, however, a bulge in the teen-age population in many European countries did not cause a bulge in the teen-age labor force. The rise in enrollment rates in upper secondary schools in Western Europe in the 1960s—a development that had occurred earlier in the United States and Canada—was so pronounced that teen-age labor force participation rates declined sharply. The rise resulted primarily from (1) an increase in the

Figure 1.6 *(continued)*

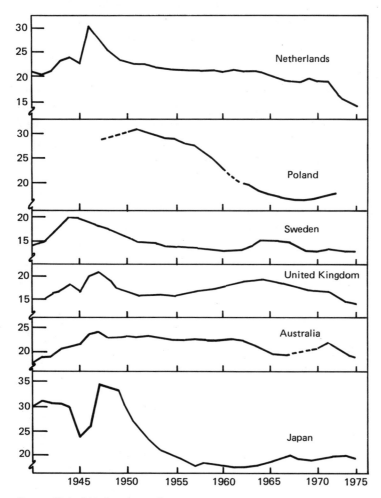

Source: United Nations (annual).

legal school–leaving age, reflecting recognition of the need for
more education to meet the labor force requirements associated
with advancing technology; (2) social and political movements
stressing greater equality of opportunity, which led to policies
to increase access to upper secondary schools and to make them
less elitist; and (3) increasing recognition by parents and their

children of the social and economic benefits of advanced education. Labor force participation rates of men (but not of women) aged 20 to 24 also tended to decline in some European countries (though not as precipitously as teen-age rates), reflecting the rise in enrollment rates in higher education, which in turn resulted from many of the same influences that were raising enrollment rates in secondary schools (Organization for Economic Cooperation and Development, Manpower and Social Affairs Committee, 1978). Increasing enrollment rates have not caused labor force participation rates to decline in the United States or Canada, where it has become increasingly common for students to seek part-time employment. However, in Western Europe, secondary school students rarely seek part-time jobs, and thus a rise in secondary school enrollment rates tends to be associated with a decline in the proportion in the labor force. University students in Europe are also considerably less likely than students in North America to work during school months, although many seek work during summer vacation.

Was the decline in labor force participation rates in Europe pronounced enough to offset the increase in the size of the youthful population? For teen-agers, the answer, in general, is yes. The prevailing trend in numbers of teen-agers in the labor force in a number of industrial countries outside the United States, Canada, and Australia was downward, at least until about 1974, when a slight reversal in this trend occurred in several countries. Among those aged 20 to 24, however, the situation was different, partly because of rising labor force participation rates of women. Although no country had as pronounced and continuous an upward trend for this age group as the United States and Canada, the situation was far more mixed than among teen-agers.[1]

The bulge in the teen-age labor force—as distinct from the teen-age population—cannot be held responsible for teen-age unemployment in most industrial countries before 1974. But in Great Britain, Sweden, and Germany there is apprehension about the current increase in the youthful population.

[1] This discussion is based on unpublished data provided by the U.S. Bureau of Labor Statistics.

Moreover, in the United States, distinguishing between white and nonwhite teen-age unemployment rates casts additional doubt on the supply hypothesis. The unemployment differential for white teen-agers rose very little in the 1960s except for males aged 16 to 17, but the nonwhite differential began to rise in the mid-1950s and rose much more sharply than the white differential in the 1960s (Figure 1.7). Why did the nonwhite differential rise in the mid-1950s?[2] The answer seems to lie largely in the migration of the black population that was stimulated by World War II and later by the Korean war. By 1950, slightly more than half of the nonwhite population aged 15 to 19 lived in urban areas, and by 1960 the proportion was nearly two-thirds. Thus, youthful nonwhites, along with adults, had been moving out of rural areas, where unemployment tends to be low (or at least hidden in the form of underemployment), to urban areas, where the competition with whites for jobs is more intense. They were also, of course, moving out of the South, although the proportion of youthful nonwhites living outside of the South did not approach one-half until the 1970 census. The newly urbanized nonwhites were undoubtedly hard hit by the recession that followed the end of the Korean war— the worsening of nonwhite-white unemployment differentials that occurred around that time affected adult as well as youthful nonwhites. As Killingsworth (1967, p. 72), in a thorough review of the relative worsening of the job situation of blacks in the 1950s and early 1960s, put it: "The trends of the past quarter century in Negro migration, birth rates, death rates, occupational shifts, and school attendance are now yielding the largest increase in Negro population in the regions and among the groups where Negro disadvantages are greatest." He went on to point out that, in view of the heavy concentration of black unemployment in the slums of large cities, a program to create jobs appeared to be the only short-run answer "that can be made to fit the size and shape of the problem."

---

[2] I shall distinguish between nonwhites and blacks alone. However, because more than 90 percent of nonwhites are black, the data for blacks and for nonwhites tend to be very similar.

Figure 1.7. **Unemployment of teen–agers by race, United States,
annual averages 1954 to 1978**

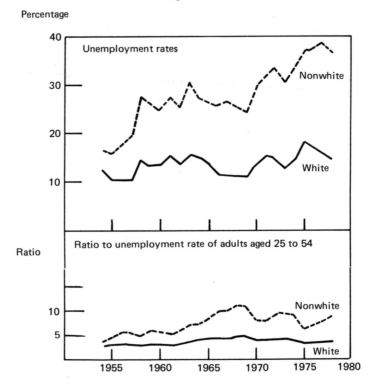

Source: *Employment and Earnings* (1979); The President (1978).

However, other aspects of the supply hypothesis must be considered. What about the competition of the large numbers of married women who have entered the labor force in recent decades and who may be getting jobs that teen–agers would have otherwise obtained? What about the competition of illegal aliens, who have entered the United States in large numbers and who also present a problem in Western Europe? What about the possibility that the sluggishness of employment in Western Europe has left a number of countries with an excess supply of foreign workers, even though work permits for many of these people have been discontinued and many have returned to their

native countries since 1973-74? And what about the competition of college and university graduates for jobs that would have
formerly gone to high school graduates or even to high school
dropouts?

The labor force participation rate of women has not risen
substantially in all Western industrial countries. It has done so
in Australia and Sweden—along with the United States and Canada—and also in Great Britain, though somewhat more moderately. On the other hand, it has remained relatively stable in
France and has declined in Japan and Italy. It also declined
slightly in Germany in the 1960s, but not recently (U.S. Bureau
of Labor Statistics, 1978, p. 43). A major factor in Italy and
Japan has been the sharp postwar decline in agricultural employment in both countries—women who were economically active
as unpaid family workers on the farm generally withdraw from
the labor force when the family moves to the city. Adult female
activity has been rising in Germany, but not enough to make up
for the sharp drop in participation of teen-age girls. In France,
the decline in self-employment, both on the farm and in the
city, probably explains the sluggishness of the female labor
force participation rate.

Suggesting that the competition of adult women has been
important, the OECD pointed out that "with but three notable
exceptions, if countries are ranked in order of their 1975 youth
unemployment rates, it can be seen that the ranking very nearly
corresponds to that which obtains when countries are ranked in
accordance with the changing labour force share of youth plus
adult females" (Organization for Economic Cooperation and
Development, 1977c, p. 15, see Table 1.1). The three exceptions were Sweden and Finland, which had relatively large increases in the youth and adult female labor forces with very
small increases in youth unemployment, and Italy, which had a
minor increase in these combined labor forces but a very large
increase in youth unemployment. Commenting that the entry
of women into the labor force is often mentioned as a potential
cause for rising youth unemployment, the report conceded that
detailed analyses of this presumed relationship do not exist and

Table 1.1. **OECD member countries ranked by percent change in
combined youth and adult female share of the labor force from
1970 through 1975 and by youth unemployment rate in 1975**

Country	Ranking by change in youth and adult female share of labor force	Ranking by youth unemployment rate
Canada	1	2
United States	2	1
Australia	2	4
Spain	3	3
Greece	4	5
United Kingdom	5	6
West Germany	6	7
Japan	7	8

Note: Rankings exclude Finland, Italy, and Sweden for reasons explained in text.
Spearman rank correlation coefficient = 0.9.

Source: Organization for Economic Cooperation and Development (1977c).

suggested that to verify this relationship would require very re-
fined data by occupation and industry of the rates of growth of
employment and wage rates of adult females and youth over
time.

The chief results of such an analysis for the United States,
based on changes from 1960 to 1970,[3] may be summarized as
follows:

1. The number of occupations in which employment
changes were relatively favorable for both women and teen-agers
(or for adult women and either teen-age boys or teen-age girls)
and in which employment changes were relatively unfavorable
for both women and teen-agers far exceeded those in which
trends for women and teen-agers differed. In general, those occupations in which total employment was expanding rapidly
were also favorable for both women and teen-agers, and con-
versely.

2. Some occupations were particularly favorable for
women and teen-age girls—primarily the clerical jobs that have

[3] This type of analysis must be based on decennial census data because
data obtained between censuses are not sufficiently detailed.

traditionally been female, such as bank tellers, file clerks, receptionists, and typists, as well as such jobs as sewers and stitchers. Certain other occupations were particularly favorable for women and teen-age boys, chiefly traditionally male occupations, such as those of shipping and receiving clerks.

3. Teen-agers fared appreciably better than adult women in some occupations, including those of cooks (probably short-order cooks), sales clerks in both general merchandise and apparel stores, waiters and waitresses, and counter and fountain workers. Teen-agers probably fared so well in these often non-unionized and unstructured trade and service occupations because they could be hired at lower wages and with fewer fringe benefits than adult women. On the other hand, women fared distinctly better than teen-agers in various types of driving jobs, including those of deliverypersons and routepersons, probably because of the much higher insurance rates for teen-agers and the presumed unreliability of teen-agers compared with women. Women also made much more spectacular percentage gains in several traditionally male occupations, such as those of auto mechanics and carpenters, although the total number of women employed in such occupations continued to be small. However, in some of the less skilled, traditionally male occupations, such as laborers in wholesale and retail trade, garage workers, and service station attendants, teen-age boys fared much better than either girls or women.

4. In general, the least favorable occupations for all these groups were in manufacturing, although increases in employment of assemblers, sewers, and stitchers during the 1960s were substantial. Also unfavorably affected were stenographers (probably because of the increased use of dictaphones, telephones, and other equipment) and clerical workers "not elsewhere classified" in various industries. Of interest also was the decline in employment in several occupations that were traditionally youth jobs, such as messengers, office boys, and newspaper deliverers.

5. Technological changes caused a number of the employment shifts that occurred, even when changing technology was not specifically mentioned.

6. Perhaps the single most impressive finding is that the occupations in which the most spectacular gains were made by

teen-agers were low paid and low-status service occupations, such as cooks, janitors, and cleaners. The part-time and often temporary character of many of these jobs undoubtedly contribute to the upward trend in teen-age unemployment rates, especially for minority-group youth. Moreover—and this is important in relation to policy issues—jobs of this type require very little training.

The companion analysis of employment changes by detailed industry classification yielded results that were generally consistent with those of the occupational analysis, especially the fact that trends for teen-agers and women were more often alike than unlike.

Without question, illegal aliens compete for jobs with youth and also with women. As Piore (1977) has indicated, recently arrived illegal immigrants expect to remain only temporarily and are content to compete for secondary jobs (in dual labor market terms), because their goal is usually to accumulate a certain amount of money and return home.

Foreign workers in Europe were hired during a period when a shortage of native-born workers, including young people, existed, and many who have not returned to their homelands now hold jobs that might otherwise be available for youth. Also, evidence clearly shows that particularly high unemployment rates are found among teen-age children of foreign workers in some European countries.

College graduates in the United States have been getting lower-level white collar, blue collar, and service jobs in the 1970s that in the 1960s would have been obtained by high school graduates and dropouts. In other words, college graduates have been "bumping" young people with less education because of the relatively unfavorable job market that has developed for college graduates in the 1970s. This deterioration of the job market stemmed from developments on both the demand side (the leveling off of federal research and development expenditures, for example, and the decline in the demand for schoolteachers) and the supply side (an exceptionally large flow of college graduates into the labor market in the 1970s).[4] But I consider the phenomenon here as a supply factor in terms of its impact on the job market for high school graduates and dropouts and for those with only a few years of college. Somewhat similarly, the competition of disappointed university aspirants for apprenticeship positions in West Germany tends to exacerbate unemployment among less educated youth.

Disaggregating American Data

Certain additional aspects of youth unemployment can be illuminated by disaggregation of American data:

1. Although labor economists have long recognized that young people shift jobs relatively frequently in their first few years in the labor force—and that this shifting helps to explain high youth unemployment rates—in 1976 less than 10 percent of unemployed persons aged 16 to 19 were out of work because of having left their last jobs. The great majority (nearly 70 percent) were jobless because they were reentering the labor force or had never worked before (The President, 1977, table A-25).

2. The search for a job by the youthful entrant or reentrant to the labor force does not usually last very long. Spells of unemployment for young people tend to be considerably shorter than for adults. However, when a recession deepens, these spells tend to lengthen for both youth and adults; this phenomenon has happened in recent years not only in the United States but also in other industrial countries (Organization for Economic Cooperation and Development, 1977c, p. 4). Canadian data also show that youthful reentrants to the labor force find jobs in considerably less time than do youthful entrants (Organization for Economic Cooperation and Development, 1977b). Moreover, young people are likely to have more frequent spells of unemployment and thus to be out of work for more weeks in any given year than adults according to annual reports of the U.S. Bureau of Labor Statistics.

[4] For a detailed analysis of these developments, see Carnegie Commission on Higher Education (1973) and Gordon (1974).

3. Unemployed youth include many students who are seeking part-time jobs. If all students aged 16 to 24 had been eliminated from the civilian labor force and from the unemployed, the national unemployment rate would have been reduced from 8.5 to 7.9 percent in 1975; however, the unemployment rate for all persons aged 16 to 24 would hardly have changed, because unemployment rates of students and nonstudents are about equal. Because students do not regard the jobs that they get while in school as having any significant relationship to their future occupational status, they are likely to be content with jobs that youthful nonstudents regard as very unsatisfactory.

4. Unemployment rates of young people (and of adults as well) are inversely related to educational attainment and are very high for high school dropouts. This type of relationship holds for virtually every country, developed and less developed, for which data exist, as the essays written for the Carnegie Council clearly indicate.

Conclusions on Causes

Youth unemployment has become far more serious in many industrial countries than at any time since the postwar readjustment period. Moreover, there is a widespread and growing agreement that restoration of full employment will not eliminate youth unemployment in most countries; in this sense the problem is only partly cyclical.

An increase in the supply of young people in the labor market played a role, though not necessarily a dominant one, in the United States and Canada in the 1960s. However, in most other industrial countries the size of the teen-age labor force declined as secondary school enrollment rates soared—a trend that has continued in a number of countries in the 1970s. But the total supply of workers was affected in several countries by a pronounced increase in labor force participation rates of adult women, by the importation of foreign workers, and, in the United States (and apparently in some European countries), by an influx of illegal aliens. Some evidence indicates that an increase in the supply of women in the labor force may have exacerbated youth unemployment in a number of countries. Our special analysis of American employment data, however, suggests that factors influencing the rate of growth or decline of total employment in individual occupations largely explain occupational changes for teen-agers from 1960 to 1970, and that the competition of women explained adverse employment experiences for youth only in a few occupations—notably jobs involving driving.

The situation that seems to be common to nearly all industrial countries is the set of forces on the demand side of the labor market that impair job opportunities for youth. These forces will remain for a long time, and they require vigorous policy measures if the youth unemployment problem is to be held within reasonable bounds. In fact, the long-run forces that have been decreasing the relative demand for young people in the labor market may well be intensified rather than reversed.

What is the outlook for the 1980s? As we have seen, the Organization for Economic Cooperation and Development does not anticipate achievement of full employment until about 1982 and predicts that, for the OECD area as a whole, excess supply will prevail in the youth labor market for several years beyond that. Clearly, however, the situation varies considerably from country to country.

In the United States and Canada, the teen-age population will be decreasing in the 1980s, and the population aged 20 to 24 will begin to decline around 1982-83. In the United States, the decline in the size of these youthful age groups is not likely to be offset by the comparatively modest increase in labor force participation rates that is anticipated, especially in the case of males, so that the overall supply of young people on the labor market will be decreasing (The President, 1977, table E-2). R. A. Gordon (1978, p. 104) has suggested that, if manpower and related programs are not substantially changed, the unemployment rate will decline significantly for teen-agers and moderately for adults aged 20 to 24. The ratio of the teen-age to the national unemployment rate is likely to decline during the 1980s according to Gordon's projections, from about three times the national rate to about two times.[5] This would mean a decided improvement for the age group as a whole; however, because their unemployment rates are so high, I foresee little improvement for inner-city blacks without more far-reaching measures than we have seen thus far. Furthermore, because of higher birth rates in the black population, the percentage of blacks in the youthful population will rise throughout the coming decade. Federal population estimates indicate that the number of whites aged 16 to 21 will decline appreciably between 1980 and 1990, while the nonwhite male population in the same age group will rise slightly. As a result, the nonwhite percentage of this age group will rise from 15.8 percent in 1980 to 18.6 percent in 1990. The youthful Hispanic population is also rising rapidly and probably will continue to do so.

In other countries the situation will vary considerably, especially because of the differences in demographic trends that we have noted. Unquestionably, a return to full employment would reduce youth unemployment rates substantially, but in Great Britain, Sweden, and Germany the current or impending increase in the youthful population may well make reducing youth unemployment differentials difficult. Moreover, in most Western European countries, an increasing proportion of young people entering the labor market will be the children of foreign workers, who are likely to have differentially high unemployment rates. Also, as already suggested, the impact of long-run structural changes reducing the relative demand for young workers could well be intensified. Thus, I conclude that few, if any, Western industrial countries can afford to be complacent about the prospect for the 1980s, assuming that the problem of youth unemployment will go away.

Policies to Combat Youth Unemployment

Policies to combat youth unemployment include not only macroeconomic policies and specific labor market policies but also

[5] The ratio of the teen-age rate to the national rate is, of course, lower than the ratio of the teen-age rate to the adult rate shown in Figure 1.1.

educational policies, which are frequently ignored. The essays written for the Carnegie Council are distinctive in devoting considerable attention to both labor market and educational policies.

Labor Market Policies

The rising trend of youth unemployment has led to many legislative measures in the last few years to combat the situation (Table 1.2). There is a certain similarity in the types of measures adopted by various industrial countries, but in many cases the programs are too new to permit evaluation of their results. Moreover, any attempt to review the existing evaluative literature would extend the length of this chapter unmanageably. I shall merely list certain policies that I believe are especially worthy of consideration outside of the countries in which they are found. Except where otherwise noted, the discussion is based on the relevant volumes in Carnegie Council (1978; 1979).

1. Denmark. Experimental residential programs for unemployed youth, which combine education, a choice of various types of work experience, and shared responsibility for providing necessary residential services.

2. Great Britain. *a.* Community Industry, sponsored by the National Association of Youth Clubs, which operates a network of enterprises staffed by young people throughout the country. It provides various kinds of goods and services that are of value to the community but that are not normally supplied by private enterprise.

b. The Careers Service (formerly the Youth Employment Service), which is entirely responsible for the placement of school leavers below the age of 18 and also usually handles those in older age groups for the first two years after they leave full-time education. The service is legally required to maintain the school-leaver unemployment register and to receive notification of vacancies, as well as to handle placement. According to Feldstein (1973, p. 10), the great majority of school leavers who do not go to higher education are interviewed in schools by the service.

c. A recently adopted comprehensive youth opportunities program for those under age 19 and usually referred by

Table 1.2. Labor market policies to combat

Country	Youth employment services[a]	Moving allowances[b]	Training programs[c]			Employer Youth only
			Institutional	Subsidized on-the-job	Apprenticeship	
Australia	xx	—	xx	xx	xxx	—
Belgium	x	—	xx	xx	xx	—
Canada	xx	xx	xxx	xx	xx	—
Denmark	xx	—	xx	x	xx	xx
France	x	x	xx	xxx	xx	xx
West Germany	x	xx	xx	x	xxx	—
Netherlands	xxx	xx	xx	xx	xx	xx
Sweden	xxx	xxx	xxx	xx	—	xx
United Kingdom	xxx	xxx	xxx	xxx	xx	xx
United States	xx	—	xx	xx	xx	x

Note: x = slight emphasis; xx = moderate emphasis; xxx = major emphasis.

[a]All countries have public employment services; indicated here, however, is the extent of special employment services, as well as counseling and guidance services, for youth.

[b]Some countries with moving allowance programs did not report any expenditures for such programs to OECD in 1977 (see Table 1.3).

[c]Also includes some career education and work orientation programs.

[d]These subsidy programs do not necessarily involve training, as do those classified under subsidized on-the-job training.

the Careers Service, providing training, work experience, and educational options, with the details of the actual projects to be planned by local committees representing community, educational, management, and trade union interests.

3. Japan. Training programs in industry that combine high school or postsecondary education and vocational training.

4. Sweden. *a.* Vocational guidance and career education in all schools, provided by specially trained full-time counselors (required to have some work experience other than teaching), for students beginning at about age 13.

b. The well-known Swedish selective labor market policies under the guidance of the National Labor Market Board, including extensive training programs, work relief, public service employment, moving allowances, and (recently) employer subsidies for hiring youth.

youth unemployment, selected countries, 1977

subsidies[d] Not confined to youth	Public service employment	Work experience programs[e]	Community work and education councils	Subsidized summer employment	Comprehensive youth opportunities program[f]	Policies to induce early retirement
—	xx	xx	—	—	—	—
xx	xx	—	—	—	—	xxx
—	xx	xx	—	xx	—	—
—	xx	xx	—	—	xx	—
—	xx	x	—	—	—	xxx
xx	xx	—	—	—	—	—
xx	xx	xx	—	—	—	x
—	xxx	xx	xxx	—	—	—
xx	xx	xxx	—	—	xxx	x
xx	xxx	xxx	xx	xxx	xx	—

[e]Includes chiefly programs of subsidized work experience with nonprofit agencies; in some cases a single program includes subsidies for both public and nonprofit employment. If so, it is classified under both public service employment and work experience programs.

[f]May overlap with other, more specialized programs.

Sources: Carnegie Council on Higher Education (1979); Organization for Economic Cooperation and Development (1977b); Booz, Allen, and Hamilton (1975); Köditz (1977a, 1977b); Reubens (1977, 1978); Schoos (1977).

Educational Policies

Unlike labor market policies, which can be adopted rather quickly, educational policies inevitably evolve slowly and cannot abruptly depart from past traditions easily. Although legal school–leaving ages do not vary greatly among industrial countries, the proportion of young people who proceed to further schooling after completing compulsory education varies enormously, as Figure 1.8 indicates. These differences are unlikely to change very rapidly.

Moreover, the educational systems in a number of countries have bottlenecks that impede progress from one level of schooling to the next, which may thus exacerbate labor market problems by forcing ill-prepared youngsters into the labor market. In comparing expenditures on manpower programs from country to country (Table 1.3), one should keep in mind the fact

Figure 1.8. Percentages of people aged 16 to 19 enrolled in educational institutions, selected countries, around 1970

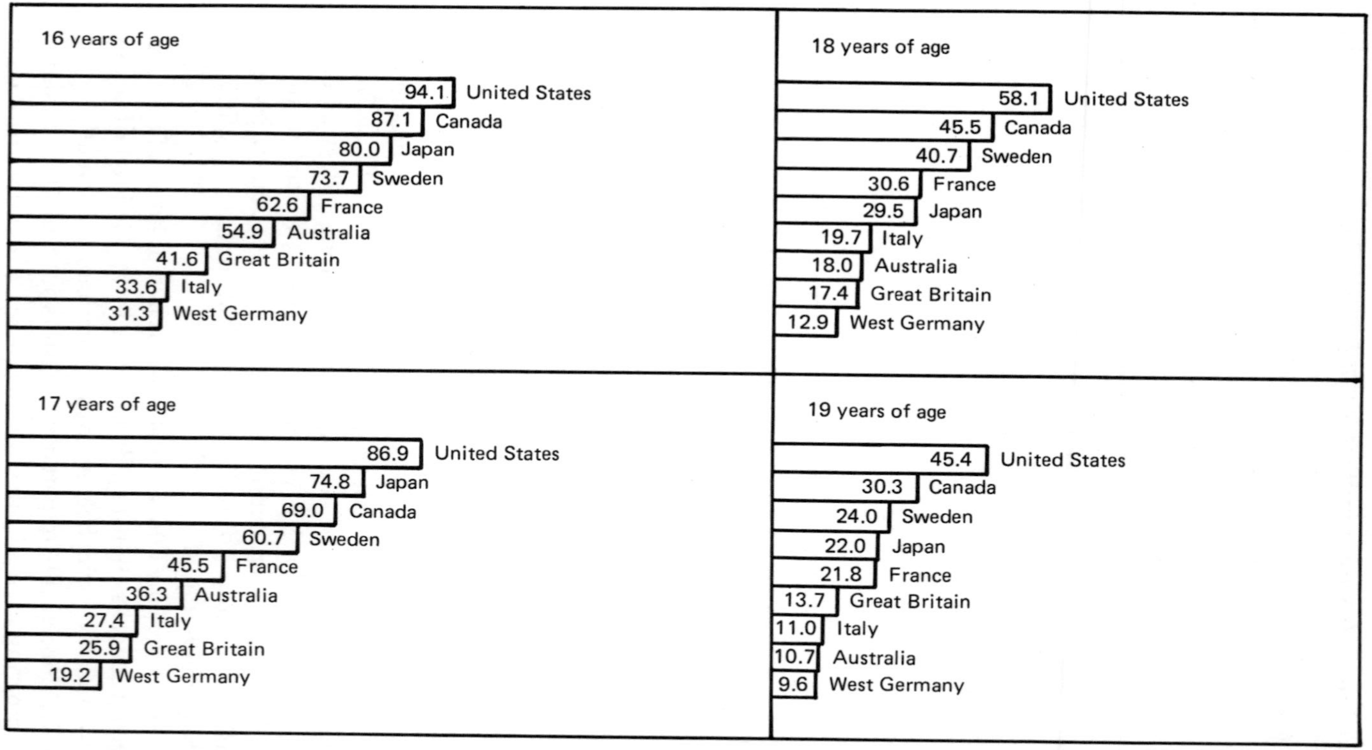

16 years of age

94.1 United States
87.1 Canada
80.0 Japan
73.7 Sweden
62.6 France
54.9 Australia
41.6 Great Britain
33.6 Italy
31.3 West Germany

17 years of age

86.9 United States
74.8 Japan
69.0 Canada
60.7 Sweden
45.5 France
36.3 Australia
27.4 Italy
25.9 Great Britain
19.2 West Germany

18 years of age

58.1 United States
45.5 Canada
40.7 Sweden
30.6 France
29.5 Japan
19.7 Italy
18.0 Australia
17.4 Great Britain
12.9 West Germany

19 years of age

45.4 United States
30.3 Canada
24.0 Sweden
22.0 Japan
21.8 France
13.7 Great Britain
11.0 Italy
10.7 Australia
9.6 West Germany

Note: Figures for the United States, Canada, Japan, France, and Great Britain are for 1970; for Italy, 1966; for West Germany, 1969. for Sweden and Australia, 1972;

Source: U.S. Bureau of Labor Statistics (1978, table 22).

Table 1.3. Public expenditures on employment and manpower policies as a percentage of gross national product, selected countries, 1975–76

Country	Total	Training	Temporary employment maintenance or creation	Geographical mobility	Employment service	Handicapped persons	Other
Australia[a]	0.34	0.11	0.18	—	0.04	—	—
Canada[b]	0.51	0.31	0.10	0.01	0.06	0.01	0.02
Denmark	1.51	0.13	1.28	—	0.04	0.05	—
France	0.28	0.20	0.02	—	0.03	0.03	—
West Germany[a,c]	0.87	0.27	0.35	—	0.19	0.04	0.01
Japan	0.72	0.02	0.01	—	—	—	0.69
Netherlands[c]	0.42	0.02	0.35	—	0.05	—	—
Sweden[b,d]	1.72	0.34	0.88	0.02	0.16	0.31	—
United Kingdom	0.63	0.17	0.22	—	0.14	—	0.10
United States[a]	0.57	0.13	0.30	—	0.03	0.05	0.06

[a]Data not specified are not included in the total.

[b]Data not specified are included in the total.

[c]Data for 1974–75.

[d]Percentage of gross domestic product.

Source: Organization for Economic Cooperation and Development (1977d).

Table 1.4. **Public expenditures on education as a percentage of gross national product, selected countries, around 1974**

Country	Percentage
Belgium	5.1
Canada	7.6
Denmark	7.8[a]
France	5.3[b]
West Germany	4.1[b]
Italy	5.4[b]
Japan	4.3[c]
Netherlands	7.8[c]
Sweden	7.7[b]
United Kingdom	6.3[b]
United States	6.6

[a]Percentage of gross domestic product.
[b]Data for 1973.
[c]Data for 1972.

Source: United Nations Educational, Scientific, and Cultural Organization (1975, table 6.1).

that educational and training opportunities for young people are also affected by relative educational expenditures (Table 1.4).

Sweden not only spends relatively more on manpower programs than any other country (according to Rehn, 1979, these expenditures now amount to more than three percent of the GNP), but also has comparatively high expenditures on education. Yet, as Rehn shows, many young people are denied admission to upper secondary schools in Sweden, and the rejection rate is particularly high for students applying to certain vocational programs designed for occupations deemed to have an actual or threatened surplus of qualified workers. Rehn rightly bemoans the short-sightedness of a policy in which the costs of reorienting young people are met by the manpower budget, when the educational system might have administered more appropriate treatment. In doing so, he displays an awareness of the trade-offs between educational and labor market policies that are not always so clearly recognized.

Other examples of disjunction between the educational system and the labor market are brought out by von Dohnanyi (1979), who is critical of the German policies that force parents and their children to decide at the end of the fourth year of schooling among three types of continuing schools—the basic school, which leads only to the so-called practical vocations, the intermediate school, which leads to technical education, or the *Gymnasium,* which alone leads to the university and to academic and professional careers. Because the choice of the basic school excludes future opportunities in the more favored types of schooling, this policy creates very strong preferences for enrollment in the intermediate schools or in the *Gymnasien* and downgrades the status of the basic schools. Moreover, students face another disjunction when they enter the university because of the limitations on entry into a number of faculties due to the so-called *numerus clausus.*

Despite all of the problems of the American educational system, especially in inner-city schools, it has few such bottlenecks. Entry into high schools is not restricted; while universities and the more elite colleges are quite selective in their admissions policies, any high school graduate can enter a community college in most states, and transfer to four-year colleges and universities is possible for students who have satisfactory community college records. Some community college systems will also admit adults who are not high school graduates. Thus, in comparing American manpower programs with the more extensive programs in some European countries, the greater openness of the American educational system must be kept in mind.

At the heart of many of the difficulties involved in developing adequate manpower and educational policies for youth is the problem of achieving greater equality of opportunity in pursuing different paths from school to work.[6] In the United States, students who go on to college can qualify for what is coming to be quite substantial student aid, but very little student aid is available at the secondary school level. Students who

[6] This will be a central issue to be considered in a forthcoming report on youth to be issued by the Carnegie Council on Policy Studies in Higher Education.

enroll in higher education usually qualify for aid in Western Europe, and a limited amount of student assistance is available at the secondary level in some European countries. Also, all industrial countries but the United States have a family allowance system—though with widely varying levels of payments—which tends to provide continued payments for students enrolled in school or college to age 21 or more. In the United States, welfare payments are available for young people continuing in school to age 21, but they are likely to be desperately needed for family consumption purposes and, for the most part, are limited to young people from broken homes. Social security payments are also available for children of retired, disabled, or deceased workers continuing in school—as they are in other industrial countries as well—but again may be very much needed for family consumption.

Against this background, the problem of providing training allowances or wages in public service or work experience programs to young people without impairing incentives to continue in school or to return to school is emerging. In his essay on Britain, Maclure (1979) points to this problem in discussing the new policy under which unemployed young people are provided a uniform allowance of £18 a week for participating in a variety of training or work experience programs. Such a stipend is considerably more than any kind of student assistance.

Another complication here is the competition of the vocational education system (usually under the ministry of education) with manpower programs for youth (usually under the ministry of labor). Probably in part because of this conflict, American manpower programs have until recently tended to emphasize work experience rather than training for people under the age of 20 or 21, and this has also been true in Sweden.

The most critical issues in educational policy relate especially to the secondary level and to the problem of improved preparation for the labor market of young people who are not going on to higher education. The most difficult problems at this level involve those students who have long since been "turned off" by school or who have not succeeded in acquiring basic literacy and what the British call "numeracy"—for example, Henri Janne's (1979) "laggers" and many minority-group youngsters in the ghetto schools of inner cities in the United States. Virtually every Western industrial country is now trying to meet these problems more effectively, and a comprehensive summary of all the relevant developments—recent and not so recent—would be beyond the scope of the present chapter.[7] I shall list a few developments that impress me as deserving parricular attention:

1. Canada. Cooperative education programs in most provinces intended for the less successful pupils in secondary schools, under which students alternate study and work. The problems involved in implementing this program are well worth noting (Organization for Economic Cooperation and Development, 1976, pp. 70-71).

2. Denmark and Sweden. Short courses for unemployed youth in upper secondary school.

3. France. *a.* The recent introduction of manual and technical training for all pupils in the "core curriculum" in the four years of secondary education (Organization for Economic Cooperation and Development, 1977b).

    b. The introduction of entrance examinations for admission to institutions of higher education for candidates who have acquired an occupational qualification in secondary education. Some 70 institutions of higher education will be open to such candidates (Organization for Economic Cooperation and Development, 1977b).

4. Great Britain. The relatively rapid development of sixth form colleges for the 16-to-19 age group, with open admissions policies and in many cases academic and vocational options resembling those of community colleges in the United States (Wheatley, 1976; Moore, 1976).

---

[7] For extensive discussions of these developments, see Organization for Economic Cooperation and Development (1976) and Institute of Education (1976).

5. West Germany. The innovative program of the upper secondary schools *(Kollegstufe)* of North Rhine-Westphalia, in which students can obtain both a vocational and an academic qualification, regardless of whether they are enrolled in primarily academic or primarily vocational programs, and in which education in any subject includes the whole spectrum of related academic disciplines (Sellin, 1976).

6. Poland. The opportunities for graduates of both academic and vocational programs in secondary schools to be admitted to institutions of higher education.

7. United States. The gradual transformation of open-door community colleges from institutions in which the majority of students were recent high school graduates entering academic (transfer) programs to institutions with a far broader mix of youthful and adult (typically part-time) students, with about as many students enrolled in occupational as in academic programs. Recently, an increasing number of community colleges have been providing vocational programs for disadvantaged unemployed youth referred by local Comprehensive Employment and Training (CETA) programs, and some of them are beginning to enroll high school students in occupational programs. The next stage may well be a more widespread and extensive merging of the occupational programs of high schools and of community colleges.

The problems common to the secondary school systems of all Western industrial countries stem in part from the prolongation of schooling, which retains many students who in an earlier era would not have proceeded beyond the primary school stage and who in many cases do not thrive on an education program that is exclusively academically oriented. In the next decade, extensive experimentation to provide a more stimulating school-work-training environment for such students is likely.

In conclusion, if youth unemployment will be a continuing problem, as the evidence seems to suggest, policies in both the labor market and educational spheres must continually be adapted to achieve greater equality of opportunity for young people.

At the same time, it must be recognized that labor market and education policies alone, without a wide spectrum of other social policies, will not solve the problems of the most severely deprived youth.

2

Comparative National Experiences

Youth education and unemployment are concerns of almost all industrial nations; they also present problems for the less developed countries. The following reviews of youth problems are based on a series of essays by experts on youth in eight countries and one important developing area. The full essays have been published separately by the Carnegie Council on Policy Studies in Higher Education. The countries included and the authors of the essays are:

- Great Britain: Stuart Maclure, editor, *The Times Educational Supplement* (London)
- West Germany: Klaus von Dohnanyi, minister of state and member of Parliament, Federal Republic of Germany
- Belgium: Henri Janne, professor of sociology, University of Brussels
- Sweden: Gösta Rehn, director, Swedish Institute for Social Research
- Denmark: K. Helveg Petersen, former minister of education and cultural affairs, Denmark
- Poland: Barbara Liberska, associate professor of sociology, University of Krakow
- Japan: Hidetoshi Kato, professor, Faculty of Law, Gakushuin University
- Mexico: Alberto Hernández Medina, chief, economics of education, Educational Research Center, and Carlos Muñoz

Izquierdo, technical director, Educational Research Center, A.C. Mexico
• South Asia: Manzoor Ahmed, associate director, educational strategy studies, International Council for Educational Development.

Great Britain

Youth Unemployment

Among the countries included in the Carnegie Council studies, Great Britain has experienced a particularly sharp rise in unemployment in recent years as well as a disproportionately large increase in youth unemployment (see Figures 1.2 and 1.5). With the unemployment rate of 16- and 17-year-olds running around 13 to 14 percent and that of 18- and 19-year-olds about 10 percent in early 1977, British rates have been well below those of comparable age groups in the United States but above those in most other Western European countries.

Although originally considered a cyclical phenomenon, the youth unemployment problem is now expected to be troublesome for some years to come. Britain experienced a rise in the birth rate from 1955 to 1964 (a second upward swing that occurred after the first sharp increase immediately following World War II; see Figure 1.6, resulting in a bulge in the youthful population that will continue into the mid-1980s). The sluggish rate of growth of the British economy and the particularly difficult problem of combating inflation in Britain are also grounds for pessimism about lowering both the overall unemployment rate and the high youth unemployment rate.

In Britain, as elsewhere, young people with poor educational qualifications are among those most vulnerable to unemployment. Moreover, in one significant respect, the youth unemployment problem in Britain resembles that in the United States: Unemployment is particularly severe among minority men and women under the age of 25, especially young West Indians. As in the United States, the problem is very serious in inner-city areas, where the minority-group population is concentrated. In some parts of London, one in four of the total unemployed is colored; in the London borough of Lewisham, a

1976 survey showed that young West Indians made up 40 percent of those registered as unemployed. Nevertheless the problem of minority–group unemployment is much less severe than in the United States, because the minority–group population, though growing, is still a small proportion of the total.

The factors that have exacerbated youth unemployment in Britain are similar to those in other industrial countries. Moreover, Britain is one of the countries, along with West Germany and Sweden, in which legislation aimed at increasing job security of adult workers is viewed as discouraging the hiring of young people. In addition, policies to hold down wage increases have 'generally raised the relative earnings of the lowest-paid workers —and therefore also of youthful workers—and, along with other aspects of wage policy, have brought the wages of young people closer to those of adults, thereby reducing employment opportunities for youth.

In a country with a strong tradition of abhorring unemployment, youth unemployment has become a major political concern of the government. At a time when expenditures on most public services are closely scrutinized, substantial funds have been made available for special programs of job creation and industrial training for youth.

Controversies over Industrial Training

One of the more significant developments of recent years has been the continuing controversy over industrial training, which has affected training and employment opportunities for youth. In Britain, vocational training, largely in the form of apprenticeships, has traditionally been regarded as the responsibility of industry rather than of the schools. The tradition resembles that in West Germany, although apprenticeships in Britain have not absorbed nearly as large a proportion of school leavers, especially girls, as in West Germany. Also, the colleges of further education in Britain have provided vocational, technical, and general courses for students aged 16 and older, chiefly in evening classes but to some extent in daytime classes, whereas vocational education has not been seen as the responsibility of the secondary schools in the postwar era (except in a few fields such as shorthand and typing).

In Britain, as in the United States, unions have traditionally followed restrictionist policies regarding apprenticeship in order to hold down the supply of skilled workers, and there have long been complaints that training is conducted on a narrow craft basis that is ill suited to technological change. Although management tends to prefer policies that increase the supply of skilled workers, the employment of new apprentices falls off sharply in recessions when hiring is cut back, resulting in shortages of skilled workers shortly after recovery is under way. Because of conflict between union and management interests, training has long been a focus of controversy in British industrial relations.

To encourage more widespread and broadly based training, the Industrial Training Act was enacted in 1964, which set up training boards for each industry and provided payroll levies on employers to finance training programs organized by the boards. Progress was made under this legislation, especially in the engineering and construction industries, in revamping training and reorganizing its relationship to colleges of further education. However, apparently due to employer pressure, the legislation was weakened in certain respects by the Employment and Training Act of 1973, which limited the levy to a maximum of 1 percent of payroll and provided for a wide range of exemptions for employers. But the 1973 legislation also established the Manpower Services Commission (MSC), which has employer, union, and public representatives, to have responsibility for manpower, employment, and training services and to supervise the work of a subordinate body, the Training Services Agency, which would have substantial funds to promote training. Meanwhile, the number of school leavers entering apprenticeships fell off somewhat in the late 1960s but rose slightly in the early 1970s.

In 1976, with a view to stimulating long-term training through apprenticeships, the MSC and the Department of Employment proposed a new program to cover the first, most expensive part of the apprentice's training course, which takes place mainly off the job in a college of further education or group training center, with the funds to be provided partly by an expanded levy on payrolls and the remainder by a government grant. But the proposal floundered in the familiar arena of conflict, with the unions supporting the scheme and employers backing away, especially after Labor Party losses in several by-elections encouraged hopes for a Conservative victory in the near future and weakened the relative union strength on the MSC.

Other Policies to Combat Youth Unemployment

Many of the policies adopted by the British government to combat youth unemployment in the last few years have been similar to those carried out in other industrial countries. However, several policy developments described below are particularly deserving of comment.

Community Industry (CI). Initially sponsored by the National Association of Youth Clubs, this was the largest of a number of voluntary projects to emerge in the early 1970s. It operates a network of enterprises throughout the country that provides various goods and services to the communities that would not normally be supplied by private enterprise. Young people working in the projects are paid wages and are expected to turn out work that meets the quality criteria of the users, who are mainly local authorities and community groups. Some of the young people, who must be under 18 years of age and who normally spend a year or more with the undertaking, are assigned to craft or educational courses during their employment. As the scheme developed, it came to be administered by a national management board representing the clubs, the Trades Union Congress, the Confederation of British Industries, and the Department of Employment. The wage cost of the young workers and their supervisors is now funded by the Department of Employment (whereas many manpower projects are funded by the MSC), while local authorities provide the sites and equipment.

Youth employment subsidies. In 1975, the government announced a scheme under which employers who hired school leavers with six weeks or less of employment were to be paid £ 5 per week for the first 26 weeks, but school leavers could not be recruited to displace existing workers. A more flexible program followed in 1976, under which a subsidy of £10 a week was payable to employers hiring individuals under age 20 who had been continuously registered as unemployed for six months. More than 30,000 school leavers were hired under the first of these schemes, but under the second the number hired (10,000) fell considerably below that contemplated in the budgetary provision for the program. Even so, the scheme was continued the following year.

The Work Experience Program (WEP). This program is of particular interest because it has no precise parallel (to the best of our knowledge) in other countries and because it is regarded in Britain as relatively successful. The program is fully subsidized, in the sense that the government pays the total compensation of young people, although the employer incurs some supervisory costs. Inaugurated by the MSC in 1976, the program allocates funds for placing unemployed young workers aged 16 to 18 in private firms or local authorities for six months or more to gain experience. Although they are considered to be neither employees nor trainees in the usual sense, the need for a planned and supervised program of induction and subsequent training is emphasized, including, whenever possible, formal instruction in general skills, either by day release for further education or through existing in-company and industrial training board facilities. Originally the MSC paid the young people a flat rate, free of tax or social security contributions, of £16 a week, which was similar to amounts then payable under other MSC training programs. This was later raised to £18 a week.

By March 1978, 60,000 young people had gone through the program, and about 40,000 could be accommodated at any given time.[1] In the early stages, large employers were urged to participate to get the program started, but the participation of small employers has steadily increased, and, by the last quarter of 1977, over 70 percent of the new places were in firms with fewer than 500 employees. This experience suggests that the

[1] This discussion is based on Lasko (1978) and Smith and Lasko (1978), rather than on the essay by Stuart Maclure in the Carnegie Council series, because it seemed particularly interesting to include some information on experience under the program (not available at the time Maclure was completing his essay).

public subsidy involved means more to small employers, whereas large employers prefer to avoid the red tape of involvement
with the government. (This situation resembles, for example,
the experience with a program conducted by the Chicago Alli-
ance of Business Manpower Services, which pools applications
to the federal government for on-the-job training subsidies and
which has found that most of the firms participating are relatively small [Robison, 1978, pp. 51-52]). It has also been found
that only about 2.3 WEP participants were employed, on the
average, per establishment, suggesting that the problem of or-
ganizing participation and supervising the participants is not
likely to be difficult for most establishments.

A follow-up survey in the fall of 1977 indicated that the
majority of the participants had either been given permanent
jobs by their WEP employers or had obtained other full-time
jobs. Although 35 percent were unemployed at the time of the
survey, the average duration of unemployment for all participants after the WEP experience was much shorter than that prevailing before participation. There were also other indications that the WEP helped participants to find jobs.

The Job Creation Program (JCP). This is a public service employment program designed to benefit communities by improving
the environment or by contributing to the solution of social and
community problems. Though not confined to youth, official
policy gives priority to the young unemployed and their training needs; regarding projects, the policy emphasizes urban re-
newal. Although JCP resembles the public service employment
programs administered under the Concentrated Employment
and Training Act (CETA) in the United States, the authoriza-
tion of projects is not the responsibility of local governmental
bodies (the "prime sponsors" in CETA), but rather of lay committees representing local employers, unions, and local authorities. These committees are headed by independent chairpersons,
who are usually people of high standing in the academic community. By March 1977, the government had expended £105
million on the program, which had provided a total of 75,000

jobs, having an average duration of 31 weeks. Most projects were sponsored by local authorities, but some were under the sponsorship of voluntary agencies.

Although opinions differ, the results have generally been considered successful. An MSC 1976 validation survey indicated that one-fifth of the participants had left to take a job during the project, while nearly half found work soon after completing the program. The main criticism is the frequent absence of a significant training component.

The Careers Service. The Careers Service, which was established in 1974 as a successor to the former Youth Employment Service, is entirely responsible for the placement of school leavers below the age of 18 and, in general, handles those in older age groups for the first two years after they leave full-time education. In addition to their central role of maintaining the school-leaver unemployment register and handling placements, the careers departments are involved in a wide range of functions in the youth employment field, including guidance and referrals to manpower programs (Reubens, 1977).

Because the service is administered by local authorities, which also control the expenditure of funds, the range of activity varies considerably in different parts of the country, but the central government has tended to increase its share of the funding in recent years.

The Youth Opportunities Program. The proliferation of separate youth programs was increasingly criticized. In the autumn of 1976, the MSC set up a special working party, under the leadership of Geoffrey Holland, to examine the feasibility of a universal guarantee of employment or training for unemployed young people, along the lines being urged by major youth organizations and other groups. The working party recommended a program for young people aged 16 to 18 under which they would be guaranteed uniform compensation of £18 a week for participating in a variety of work experience or training programs. A number of existing programs, including WEP, would be merged in the new scheme. Only those who had been unemployed six weeks or more would be eligible, and a separate, temporary employment program was recommended for young people over age 19. The government committed itself to the working party's proposals in June 1977. The program for those aged 16 to 18 was funded to provide for a maximum of 234,000 young people a year, or about one-half of the commission's forecast of unemployment in this age group in 1978. The program was to have about 130,000 places at any given time.

The commission estimated that the gross cost of its program for a full year would be £168.5 million (in 1976 pounds), compared with an existing commitment to spend £105 million on programs for the young in 1977-78, but that resulting savings in social security benefits and other expenditures would bring the net cost down to around £95 million. Also, the commission indicated that parts of the program would qualify for aid from the European Social Fund. Although the scope of the program did not satisfy some of the youth organizations, the cost of a fully comprehensive scheme was deemed prohibitive.

The provision for a uniform compensation rate of £18 a week is intended to eliminate any element of financial advantage of one program over another that might affect the young person's choice. Yet it poses a serious dilemma, which Maclure (1979, pp. 12-13) expresses as follows:

> Most obviously, the work-experience program is likely to affect teenage economics: each boy or girl accepted into a work-experience scheme will qualify at once for £18 a week—considerably more than the educational maintenance allowances offered by education authorities to children from poor families who remain in school or college beyond the age of 16. Concern has been expressed by the Manpower Services Commission and the Department of Education and Science about the difficulties this may cause when children who take advantage of a work-experience opportunity later recognize the need to return to full-time education. Widespread development of work-experience schemes could lead to recurrent education

and easier two-way transit between the worlds of work and education, but not unless this financial barrier can be bridged.

Issues in British Education

Along with other countries of Western Europe, Britain has taken decisive steps toward a more egalitarian educational system in the postwar period, replacing the elitist system that prevailed before the war. Some of the most important changes have affected secondary education. The pre–1944 system provided for nine years of compulsory education, beginning at age 5 and continuing to age 14. But at age 11, before the compulsory phase was completed, those who were successful in a scholarship examination, plus those who could satisfy a minimum entrance standard and whose parents chose to pay the necessary fees, transferred to publicly supported grammar schools. Only those who were admitted to grammar schools were prepared for university entrance, and only a small fraction of the grammar school students actually entered universities.

The 1944 Education Act raised the minimum school-leaving age to 15 (to be effective in 1947 and to be succeeded by an increase to age 16 in 1973), provided that all students were to transfer to secondary schools at age 11, and abolished all fees in the secondary schools. But two groups of secondary schools were maintained: (1) the grammar schools, which took roughly the top 25 percent in terms of IQ, and (2) the modern schools, which took all the rest. Local authorities conducted eleven-plus examinations to determine which children should go to which schools. Because success in these examinations tended to be correlated with socioeconomic status, the system was far from egalitarian, but the numbers completing secondary education rose steadily after 1950, as did the numbers staying on beyond the minimum school-leaving age.

However, there had long been pressure from the Labor Party to establish comprehensive secondary schools that would admit everybody, and in the 1960s rapid progress was made in this direction. In 1966 about a quarter of all secondary school

children were in comprehensive schools, and by 1976 the proportion had risen to three-fourths. The Education Act of 1976,
opposed by the Conservatives, made the transition to comprehensive schools mandatory. Meanwhile, at least in part because
of growing concern about youth unemployment and complaints
about young people being unprepared for work, the debate has
shifted, as elsewhere, to a concern over educational standards
and the links between education and the world of work.

In postsecondary education there has also been a trend
toward more egalitarianism in recent decades. The development
of the nonuniversity sector of higher education was a major
phenomenon between 1963 and 1972. This movement involved
the expansion of both the colleges of education and the colleges
of further education, along with the designation of some of the
latter as "polytechnics," which offered an alternative to the universities for degree students. However, the attempt to encourage
the development of professional training in the polytechnics has
been only partially successful.

In the 1970s the rise in enrollment rates in British higher
education has slowed down—no doubt in part because of the less
favorable job market for graduates—and British higher education
is also facing a leveling off or even a decline in enrollment because of the impending fall in the size of the college-age population. These trends are like those in the United States and in
other Western countries; furthermore, in Britain, as elsewhere,
the need to encourage enrollment of adults in postsecondary
education in the 1980s is much discussed. Although the movement for "recurrent education" has not gone as far in Britain as
in Scandinavia or in France, the British have made their own
important contribution to adult education through the Open
University (OU), which has inspired similar programs in the
United States and elsewhere. While acknowledging that those
who enroll are likely to be in middle-class rather than in working-class occupations (to the disappointment of Labor Party
members who promoted the idea of the OU), the OU points
out that, in terms of father's occupation, the enrollees have a
much more working-class complexion.

Social and Cultural Changes

One of the prominent sociological phenomena in Britain, which finds its parallel in nearly all of the countries included in this study, is the shift from student activism in the 1960s to the relative quiet of the 1970s. At the same time, social mores have become more permissive, which has affected youth within the broader society and nonyouth as well.

Meanwhile, the rise in juvenile crime has been more pronounced than the rise in crime throughout society, and many observers link the phenomenon to growing alienation of young people. Although statistics are unreliable, hard–drug use is currently increasing, with the number of marijuana offenses going down and those involving more dangerous drugs going up—partly reflecting the fact that marijuana use is much more widely accepted. Alcohol consumption has also risen markedly among youth as well as among adults.

Unemployment and the Welfare State

The British case is pertinent to the allegation, which is frequently made in advanced countries, that unemployment in general and youth unemployment in particular are at least partially attributable to the cash payments and subsidies provided by the welfare state, which make subsistence easy. However, in most Western industrial countries, many youthful unemployed do not qualify for unemployment insurance because they have not been employed long enough to meet the eligibility conditions, but a young unemployed person in Great Britain can qualify for supplementary unemployment benefits that are paid on the basis of need without any qualifying period of employment. This has undoubtedly increased the incentive for young people to register as unemployed and may have encouraged waiting until an acceptable job turns up as well as an alternating pattern of work and unemployment. However, a survey conducted by the MSC showed that most unemployed young people were actively seeking jobs, that 40 percent of those interviewed had applied for more than six jobs, and that very few had refused a job offer. But the survey also showed that "about half the employers believe that the caliber of young people has deteriorated over the past five years in terms of their motivation and basic education."

Issues for the Future

Although many changes are under discussion, any substantial change in education and training for the 18-to-24 age group besides gradual, evolutionary changes seems unlikely for some time to come, according to Maclure. At the 16-to-19 level, however, there are many more signs of movement. If the MSC philosophy prevails, it will not be possible in the long run to offer a guarantee of training or employment without extending it to all, but this raises basic questions about the relationship between education and manpower policies that are far from resolved. What will be the relative incentives to remain in school versus participating in manpower programs, and what will be the relationships between local manpower programs and local school systems? With more part-time education, more passage in and out of school and in and out of work experience, the case for a new and essentially more adventurous approach to recurrent education is strong. And yet this whole range of issues cannot be divorced from the urgent need to improve productivity in the British economy, and any design for improving the induction of young people from school into work must consider these issues.

West Germany

The phenomenal economic growth of West Germany in the postwar period has often been characterized as an "economic miracle." In this environment of rapid growth, the unemployment rate was extraordinarily low from the mid-1950s to 1973-74, falling below 1.0 percent during much of the 1960s. Nor was youth unemployment a problem, thanks in part to the traditional emphasis on apprenticeship as the predominant means of providing vocational education to the large proportion of German youth who left school after completing compulsory education (ending at age 14 in the early part of the period and gradually raised to 15 in many of the German states later on).

A young person was likely to remain in an apprenticeship for about three years at an age when young school leavers in many other countries were shifting jobs frequently.

From 1973-74 on, the Federal Republic, along with other industrial countries, experienced a slowing of growth and a rise in the unemployment rate. By comparison, however, German unemployment rates seem very modest. Even at its peak in 1975, the overall German unemployment rate averaged only 3.7 percent and the unemployment rate of those under 20 only 6.6 percent (adjusted to U.S. concepts; U.S. Bureau of Labor Statistics, 1978, pp. 19, 35). Nevertheless, these rates seemed unacceptably high in the Federal Republic, where full employment would have been defined in the late 1960s as an unemployment rate of no more than 2 percent.

The development of a youth unemployment problem came as a surprise to the federal government. An important reason for the trend, according to the Federal Labor Institute, was the increase in regulations designed to protect the job security of mature workers, which has resulted in a redistribution of the unemployment risk.

The official statistics probably understate the extent of youth unemployment. Unemployed youths often do not register for employment with the public employment service, since they frequently have not been employed long enough to qualify for unemployment insurance. Also, many do not register because they do not believe that they can find a suitable job—they become part of the "silent reserve" or of the pool of "discouraged workers," in U.S. terminology. Another reason for possible understatement of the youth unemployment rate is that unplaced applicants for training positions are not counted as unemployed. In addition, many girls aged 15 to 17 who cannot find work simply stay at home rather than register as unemployed.

Moreover, as in Britain, the number of unemployed young people is likely to increase, primarily because those born in the period of high birth rates—from about 1955 to 1963, which is somewhat later than the period in most other industrial countries—are entering the labor market. In fact, the number of school leavers has been projected to rise from 780,000 in 1975 to 952,000 in 1981 and then to decline.

Unemployed youth, as elsewhere, tend to come from the more disadvantaged socioeconomic classes. They also come from those with less schooling. About one-third of unemployed young people have not graduated from lower secondary schools, while the unemployment rate is much higher for those who have not completed vocational training than for those who have. In the Federal Republic, moreover, as in some of the other countries of Western Europe, the unemployment rate has been higher for young women than for young men.

Measures to combat youth unemployment in the Federal Republic have been less extensive than in many other industrial countries, and they have tended to center around vocational education in general and the apprenticeship system in particular. This is not surprising in view of the relatively modest dimensions of the youth unemployment problem and the long-standing confidence in the apprenticeship system.

In general, the government has emphasized macroeconomic policies aimed at restoring full employment, rather than special measures aimed at youth. There have also been policies such as restrictions on the recruitment of foreign workers and the refusal to renew expiring foreign labor contracts, which have been aimed at improving the general labor market situation. However, measures that would favor youth in the labor market at the expense of adults have been ruled out.

Changes in Apprenticeship

In view of the important role played by the apprenticeship system, trends in the availability of training positions are crucial to understanding the youth employment situation in the Federal Republic. The traditional "dual" system, in which the youth or the parents enter into a contract with the training firm, was reinstated after World War II. The young people receive compensation from the firm, and the apprenticeship usually lasts for three years. Trainees are obliged to attend public vocational school for 6 to 12 hours a week, depending on their state of residence.

From 1967 to 1976, the total number of training positions declined somewhat, although this trend was apparently reversed in 1977. The excess supply of apprenticeships, which had prevailed from 1950 on, has disappeared. What were the reasons for this decline in the supply of apprenticeships? The following factors played a role:

1. Scientific developments have made it necessary for an increasing part of education to be theoretical and less practical, which has reduced the usefulness of apprentices for profitable business activities. Related to this development is the fact that training for occupations requiring increasingly theoretical and technical knowledge that cannot be supplied by individual firms must be provided by training institutions outside of firms. Such training positions are expensive and cannot be financed by smaller firms. Moreover, especially after 1973, the need for trained junior staff gradually decreased because the demand for workers in the manufacturing sector was declining. This was also true in certain service sectors, such as trade and finance, in which technological progress and resulting structural changes, such as supermarkets and computerized accounting, have eliminated an enormous number of jobs.

2. In the 1960s a number of state governments investigated the quality of vocational training and found it very poor. The result was the Vocational Training Law of 1969, which raised legal standards for the quality of training, strengthened the rights of apprentices, and raised the cost of training, thereby making training less profitable for employers.

3. Training costs also increased because the compensation of apprentices, especially of first-year apprentices, rose proportionately more than the earnings of skilled workers.

Meanwhile, another development made the competition for apprenticeships more difficult for those with limited education—limitations on admissions to universities, which were not increasing their capacity enough to accommodate the increasing demand for student places (discussed more fully below). As a result, graduates of secondary schools sometimes accepted apprenticeship positions while waiting for possible later admission to universities, thereby edging out applicants with less education.

When the shortage of apprenticeships became clear, a commission appointed by the federal government (the Edding Commission) looked into the financing of apprenticeship costs and concluded that small firms were bearing a disproportionate share of the expense, because a significant number of trainees received their training in small firms and then went to work for larger ones. The commission recommended a general payroll levy on all firms to provide funds to finance training positions, but legislation to implement a modified version of this recommendation did not pass. Later a bill that would have imposed the levy only on firms with a payroll of more than 400,000 DM a year was enacted, but it was heavily attacked by employers. Firms engaged in training agreed, however, to assume the responsibility for adding 100,000 training positions in 1977, and the federal government dispensed with the levy.

In recent years, federal and state public agencies have also increased the number of their training positions beyond those actually required for the training of junior staff. These developments were evidently responsible for the 1977 reversal in the downward trend in the number of training positions. They are also interesting in the light of similar employer opposition to general payroll levies to finance training in Great Britain.

Educational Issues

The educational attainment of youth has risen significantly since around 1960 in the Federal Republic, as it has in other countries of Western Europe. The percentage of young people aged 15 to 19 enrolled in upper secondary schools rose from 11 percent in 1960 to slightly over 14 percent in 1970 and to nearly 19 percent in 1975. Meanwhile, university enrollment also expanded rapidly, but not enough to accommodate the rising number of graduates of the *Gymnasien* (academic secondary schools) in the 1970s.

In addition to the problem of admission to the universities, unresolved educational issues exist, some of which are closely related to youth unemployment problems. The educational system forces choices among educational "streams" at an early age, and shifting to a different stream later on is almost impossible. After the four-year primary school (six years in Bremen and West Berlin), a student chooses among three types of lower secondary schools: (1) the basic school *(Hauptschule),* which leads directly to work, an apprenticeship, or, in some cases, a full-time vocational school; (2) a modern secondary or intermediate school *(Realschule),* which leads to an intermediate degree and then to an upper technical school; and (3) the *Gymnasium,* which leads as a rule to the matriculation examination *(Abitur)* and then to the university and to an academic or professional career.

In general, children of upper- and middle-income families choose either the *Realschule* or the *Gymnasium,* although particularly able children from socially disadvantaged backgrounds have also traditionally been admitted to the *Gymnasium.* Those who do not choose the *Gymnasium* are essentially permanently blocked from a professional career, while many of those who do choose it find cutthroat competition for the best grades to assure entry into the university.

Because the number of pupils choosing the *Gymnasium* and the *Realschule* increased sharply, there was a strong movement to increase the capacity of these schools, while the basic schools became repositories for less gifted and socially disadvantaged children, especially in urban areas. In areas with a high concentration of children of foreign workers, German-speaking children may not even form a majority of a school class. Meanwhile, in the 1960s, the need for expansion of vocational training tended to be neglected. As a result, a problem of unemployed teachers, lawyers, chemists, and engineers has developed, while unfilled jobs in trade and crafts lack trained new recruits.

To solve the problems of vocational training, many observers believe that the basic school must be upgraded. This would require making its educational standards at the lower secondary level comparable to those of the *Gymnasium,* which would allow the school types to merge, with comprehensive secondary schools replacing the three-level school system.

In recent decades, the debate over education reforms in the Federal Republic has focused on this goal. Yet such a movement, largely or fully accomplished in such countries as Great Britain and Sweden, remains a matter of controversy, with opposition from well-to-do parents of *Gymnasium* students. In the words of the author, "the antiquated and inexpedient three-level school system, with its apparently clear options and yet obvious occupational insecurities, has become a source of insecurity and depression for today's youth, which will make a future-oriented and self-assured development in democratic equality of opportunity much more difficult, if not impossible."

Another problem is the qualitative inadequacy of the vocational schools that must be attended by youths aged 15 to 18 who do not go to full-time schools. In addition, vocational/technical schools are lacking at the upper secondary level, a situation that, according to von Dohnanyi, is "definitely a cause of youth unemployment." The expansion of this type of school was provided for in the joint plan for education proposed in 1973 by the Federal-State Commission for Educational Planning (Bund-Länder Kommission für Bildungsplanung) and later approved by the federal and state governments. About 300,000 youths are enrolled in these schools, but capacity must be expanded.

Educational Policies and Youth Unemployment

Concern over youth unemployment has made certain types of educational reforms more urgent. In November 1976, the federal-state commission adopted a "program for the realization of urgent measures for the reduction of unemployment risks of youth" that was accepted by all the states.

The prolongation of schooling. Although not fully adopted as one of the measures to combat youth unemployment, there are demands for a tenth compulsory school year, primarily to reduce the supply of young people on the labor market. Yet the form that this tenth year should take has not been resolved; considerable support exists for a vocational, rather than a general, orientation, on the ground that youths of 15 or 16 generally show a high degree of "school-weariness" and could be kept in a general education program only reluctantly and without progress.

Student places at the universities. Although some view unemployment among university graduates as a reason for not expanding the number of student places in universities, the federal government advocates increased admissions to universities in view of the possibility of a continuing and probably increasing problem of youth unemployment. Expansion is viewed not only as a policy for the universities but also as part of a total educational strategy, because those *Gymnasium* graduates who are waiting to be admitted to universities represent dangerous competitors for other youth with less education. This view is supported with full realization that the additional student places will probably not be needed after about 1990, when the university-age population will decline.

Improving existing qualifications. One of the paradoxes in the Federal Republic is that, in spite of the surplus of job seekers, private industry has numerous vacancies that cannot be filled because of a dearth of qualified applicants. To help meet this problem, almost all of the states have adopted programs to encourage those who have dropped out of basic school to return to school for graduation. The courses last from four to six months and are available for all youths, regardless of age. As suggested earlier, a full-time vocational school year is being seriously considered for those who have completed basic school, and there is much interest in the program adopted in North Rhine-Westphalia, which is designed, among other things, to expose the young person to several vocational fields to encourage a more informed occupational choice.

Counseling services. The Federal Republic is also emphasizing a policy to expand counseling services, both within the schools and in the labor market, under the auspices of the Federal Labor Institute and the local chambers of industry and commerce.

Unemployment and Juvenile Delinquency

The view that youth unemployment encourages juvenile delinquency is widely held and helps to explain the vigor with which

many governments in advanced countries have moved to combat youth unemployment in recent years. Yet many social
scientists argue that no empirical evidence supports this hypothesis and that, in fact, the causal relationship runs in the other
direction—those who are prone to juvenile delinquency are especially likely to experience unemployment. In the light of this
debate, statistics and special studies discussed by von Dohnanyi
are of particular interest.

The data show that juvenile delinquency rates, at least for
most types of offenses, tended to fall in the 1970s, whereas
they rose in the more prosperous 1960s. Intensive analyses of
statistics in Munich and Duisburg-Hamburg have also shown a
clear tendency for delinquency rates to decline as youth unemployment rates rose in the 1970s. Other studies have indicated
that a connection exists between the impulse to form gangs and
to engage in crime and that the members of gangs are economically, socially, and educationally on the lowest rung of the social structure. On the other hand, young people who are affected
by rising youth unemployment rates feel stigmatized, excluded
from work, and quite disinclined toward deviant behavior, which
would push them farther into the role of an outsider. As to
drinking, unemployed youths show the typical behavior of
working youths, which includes two or three glasses of beer a
day. They cannot afford any kind of escape into alcohol. However, there are smaller groups of unemployed youth who adopt
more extreme attitudes—ranging from those who are especially
active and confident to those who are apathetic and resigned.
There is also evidence that the lack of a training position or a
job affects the self-confidence of unemployed male youth more
gravely than that of young women. Thus, while young men strive
to adjust by improving work and qualification requirements
during a period of unemployment, young women tend to adapt
by reverting to the traditional role of wife and mother.

Von Dohnanyi stresses the tentative nature of these findings, recognizing that the experience in the Federal Republic is
too recent to permit firm conclusions on the possible effects of
prolonged unemployment on young people.

Social Aspects

In the Federal Republic, the age when the race begins for better opportunities in education and employment has progressively shifted back from the time of entry into working life to early youth and even childhood. The social stress associated with admission to certain educational fields has already begun to influence the lives of children negatively. (In this respect, the situation in the Federal Republic resembles that in Japan, though it is less severe.)

During the 1960s and early 1970s, youth in the Federal Republic, as in most industrial societies, developed a measure of independence, self–assurance, and joy of living that was unknown before. A changing system of values placed love, friendship, and comradeship in the foreground. Work and making a living became secondary.

These tendencies were encouraged by financial and legal policies favorable to youth, such as complete equality for illegitimate children, essential improvements in youth labor laws, financial aid for children, and the introduction of broad financial aid in education. The attainment of majority of 18–year–olds must also be mentioned. In spite of general compulsory military service, the rights of convinced pacifists also became respected.

The rise of crime among youth in the Federal Republic has been relatively minor. Relative delinquency of those aged 14 to 17 increased only slightly between 1960 and 1975, and the same was true for those aged 18 to 20. However, there has been no increase since the early 1970s. Although alcohol consumption among youth has increased, per capita consumption of alcohol in the country has risen in general. The hard core of drug consumers among youths aged 14 to 24 is considered to be about 40,000 (50,000 on the basis of some estimates). The latter figure would amount to about 0.5 percent of the population in this age group. The percentage of addictions to hard drugs is apparently rising, while "mild drugs" and alcohol are used interchangeably, but no exact statistics are available.

The total picture of youths 15 to 24 in the Federal Republic in no way suggests a crisis.

Dangers for the Future of Youth

Despite the relatively mild character of the youth unemployment problem in the Federal Republic, certain trends in industrial societies have increasingly negative effects on the personal development of the individual, which are stressed in the author's conclusions. On the one hand, the negative effects of growth and well-being of industrial societies, for example, on the environment, are recognized by youth; on the other hand, the world economic crisis of the 1970s is viewed as only an acute phase in long-term social and economic developments that have had especially difficult consequences for youth. After a period in which general expectations of life in industrial countries rose year after year, the rights of minorities improved, class barriers were lessened, and democratic rights deepened, a general disenchantment with progress appeared, which especially affected youth.

Specifically the author warns of future problems that may develop as the sons and daughters of foreign workers form a larger percentage of the young people entering the labor force in the Federal Republic. They are likely to be particularly susceptible to unemployment, and the dangers of radicalization under conditions of long-term unemployment, especially for those with language difficulties and social isolation, are obvious. This is particularly relevant where foreign workers live under unfavorable conditions and a geographical concentration of underprivileged persons results. This problem, he concludes, must be carefully attended to in the coming years.

Belgium

Youth Unemployment

Throughout the 1960s and 1970s, the unemployment rate in Belgium was very low, but with the onset of the recession in 1974, the unemployment rate rose sharply, with a sharp increase in unemployment among the young (Figure 1.5).

The situation in the 1970s may be contrasted with that in the 1950s and early 1960s, when unemployment in Belgium was heavily concentrated among older persons. Indeed, in 1963, three-fourths of unemployed men and nearly one-half of unemployed women in Belgium were in the 50-to-65 age group (Gordon, 1965, p. 92). Data for 1976, however, show that much smaller proportions of the unemployed were in this older age group, whereas about one-fourth of the unemployed men and nearly two-fifths of the unemployed women were under 25. Moreover, unemployment among young women showed an upward trend that appeared to be structural in nature, whereas unemployment of young men was quite responsive to the business cycle.

The public in Belgium has been shocked by the rise in youth unemployment, perhaps in part because high unemployment among young people is so contrary to the earlier postwar experience. Nevertheless, the man in the street tends to think that young people have less aptitude for work than adults, and yet data compiled by the National Council for Work shows the opposite to be the case.

In Belgium, youth unemployment conforms to the familiar pattern of being heavily concentrated among those with relatively little educational attainment. In 1975, among unemployed persons under 25 years of age, 46 percent of the men and 40 percent of the women had not gone beyond primary school, and some had not even completed that stage. Another 25 percent of the men and 20 percent of the women had experienced some lower secondary education. University graduates comprised only 2.4 percent of the unemployed men and 1.2 percent of the unemployed women, but there was considerable consternation over the increases that had occurred in these percentages since 1970.

Combating Youth Unemployment

On the whole, the measures adopted in Belgium to combat youth unemployment have not been very extensive, at least by comparison with policies in Great Britain and Sweden. Instead, general antirecession policies have been emphasized.

Centers for vocational readaptation. Belgium has long had a network of centers for retraining the unemployed, in which the subsistence costs of learners are covered by unemployment insurance. These centers were used disproportionately by unemployed youth, but gradually it became apparent that unemployed young people needed more individualized care and guidance than unemployed adults. Accordingly, in 1974, the National Office of Employment created "special centers for the observation and orientation of the young unemployed." Under the program, these centers first test the skills and aspirations of the young and adapt them to possible job opportunities, if possible, with minimal cost in time and effort. The second step consists of measures designed to increase motivation. If these measures prove insufficient, the youngster proceeds to the third step, which determines the specific studies and training that the individual should follow in a regular vocational center. At this stage, also, the possibility of probationary employment in a private firm or in public service is investigated.

Although this program appears promising, it is too early to evaluate its results. It must also be recognized, according to Janne, that the most successful vocational training cannot create more jobs.

Probationary employment. A second program adopted by the Belgian government was designed to encourage both public agencies and private firms to hire young people on a probationary basis. However, inadequate appropriations prevented public agencies from emphasizing the program, while private firms were reluctant to take on unneeded workers in a period of retrenchment. Therefore, the government decided to make the program compulsory under a law of March 30, 1976 (the economic recovery law), which provided, among other things, that all private firms and public services employing more than 100 workers must hire probationers in numbers amounting to 1 percent of their total employment, with compensation amounting to between unemployment insurance and normal pay. The probationers must be under 30 years of age, never have been employed before, and holders of degrees awarded at the end of regular studies.

The effectiveness of this program is not yet clear, although the general impression is that results have not come up to expectations. Moreover, the trade unions oppose this program because they fear that the law will result in illegally low compensation for the probationers.

Bridges between study and work. A variety of measures have been adopted to create more effective links between education and work. These include the establishment of a center for research and information on studies and work and efforts by the regional committees on unemployment to improve vocational training and make it more adaptable to technological change.

Education and the Social Structure

The Belgian contribution to the Carnegie Council series, by one of Europe's leading sociologists, is notable for its wealth of information on the influence of socioeconomic status on the educational performance of students. Moreover, the data are of special interest in the United States because they demonstrate the severity of the educational handicaps experienced by children from disadvantaged backgrounds even in a country where racial differences are largely nonexistent.

Progress in the educational attainment of young people in Belgium in the postwar period has been similar to that in other European countries and requires no special comment. However, the fluctuations in enrollment in higher education since 1968 are of particular interest. Following the "hot May" of student unrest in Belgium in 1968, which was a response to similar events in Paris, the rate of increase of new entrants in Belgian universities slowed temporarily while enrollment rose sharply in the nonuniversity sector of higher education, which prepares students for various professional and technical occupations. Apparently students and their parents became somewhat wary of the universities after the turmoil of the previous spring. However, the reaction was short-lived, and university enrollment then increased rapidly again until the early stages of the recession, when poor employment prospects for university graduates appeared to discourage university enrollment but to stimulate enrollment in the nonuniversity sector.

After two years of economic recession, however, attitudes appear to have changed. Many young people prefer to enter the universities rather than register as unemployed, and the rate of increase in new enrollments has risen again. In other words, according to Janne, the universities are performing a "parking" function, giving students a place to spend their time while waiting for an improvement in the employment situation. Janne points out that the recent study by Hecquet, Verniers, and Cerych (1976) identified a similar jump in enrollment in 1975 in France, The Netherlands, Great Britain, and Sweden. Also, the increase in enrollment in higher education in the United States in 1975 (about 9 percent) exceeded that of any other year in the 1970s and was widely interpreted as a response of new entrants to a particularly high unemployment rate among recent high school graduates. These findings cast considerable doubt on the contentions of Freeman (1976) and of Dresch (1977) that an adverse job market for college graduates will inevitably depress enrollment in higher education.

Although the rise in educational attainment of young people in Belgium in the postwar period has been pronounced, the number of pupils who are held back because of lagging progress is shockingly large. For example, many in the 15-to-18 age group, who should normally be in upper secondary school, are actually enrolled in lower secondary schools, in which pupils are primarily in the 12-to-14 age group. Moreover, the phenomenon of "laggers" actually begins in the first year of primary school, in which about one-fifth of the pupils are held back, and laggers constitute 40 percent of all the pupils in the sixth grade (the last year of primary school).

A recent study, based on a survey of 37,000 pupils in the French-speaking schools in Belgium, sheds a great deal of light on the relationship between social origins and progress in the schools. (The relationship between socioeconomic status and education in the Dutch-speaking schools is likely to be similar to that in the French-speaking schools because the participation rates of pupils in the northern, or Dutch-speaking, areas of the country and in the southern, or French-speaking, areas hardly differ. Formerly, the northern areas were relatively backward in this respect.)

Among the laggers in primary school, one-fourth in the first year and 43 percent in the sixth year are sons and daughters of unskilled workers. On the other hand, the percentages who are children of top professional and managerial workers are very small. In other words, the chances of falling behind are five times greater in the first year and four times greater in the sixth year for children of unskilled workers than for those whose fathers are at the top of the occupational ladder, in spite of efforts of the schools to promote as many pupils as possible. Significant also is the fact that, in the sixth year, the children of teachers do almost as well as the children of the top professional and managerial workers. This suggests that the primary factors are the cultural level and motivation of the families more than their income level.

These general relationships between social origins and progress in schools continue at the lower secondary level. The end of the lower secondary level in Belgium marks the end of compulsory schooling (at age 15), and at this point many of those from lower-income groups go to work or enter into an apprenticeship. The laggers among the sons and daughters of high and medium staff will be forced to continue, with longer and longer delays, in the upper general secondary level. In fact, at this level, the percentages of laggers do not vary greatly among socioeconomic groups because of the weeding-out process that occurs earlier; thus, only the more able pupils from the lower-income groups persist.

What is striking is the high percentage of laggers in these schools. In the first year of the upper secondary schools, the percentage of laggers tends to run around 40 percent or more regardless of the social backgrounds of the pupils, although the percentages are somewhat lower for children of teachers, "lower staff," and agriculture than for those from other backgrounds. The percentages of laggers are much higher in the technical and vocational upper secondary schools, running around 60 percent. Children from lower-income groups tend to choose these schools. As Janne puts it, "these streams are second-rate studies for second-rate pupils." However, at the upper secondary level, the percentages of laggers tend to decline from the first to the third year, as those who have fallen behind drop out.

As another indication of the influence of social origins on education, the so-called noble streams within the general upper-secondary schools, which include Latin, mathematics, and the sciences, attract the children of high staff people, lawyers, physicians, teachers, and medium staff people, whereas the majority of children in other sociooccupational groups are in the less noble streams. The noble sections tend to lead to the university, while the less noble ones are more likely to lead to the nonuniversity sector of higher education or to such occupations as retailing and small business.

Differentiation continues within the university, with social origins playing a role in the selection of fields of study. Those from higher occupational groups tend to choose programs leading to high staff and technical positions (engineering and business) or to the "liberal" professions (medicine and law). Many of these people will fall under the technical and management category in Belgian society; although conscious of failures and injustices in its structures, they are not basically critics of the existing order. Students in other fields of studies, who often become secondary school teachers, tend to be from middle-class and, in some cases, working-class origins. They know that they are being trained for a vocational status lower in earnings and prestige than that anticipated by students in law, engineering, and medicine. They are very receptive to the message of the social sciences, in which they take courses that are common to a number of fields. This message, which tends to criticize the established order, becomes transmitted to youth once these students become teachers, especially at the upper secondary level. The impact of this phenomenon has been perceptible in Belgium since the 1950s and was important to the incidents of 1968.

Attitudes of Belgian Youth

Another highly significant study, conducted in 1969, provided survey data on the attitudes of young people aged 16 to 18 in Belgium. Although the study was carried out at a time of student unrest, when there was much discussion of the "generation gap," the results showed that young people tended to be satisfied with their relations with parents. A decided majority indicated that "my parents are able to understand my worries," while an even larger percentage agreed that they were free to make their own decisions about their companions, the use of their leisure time, and so on. The great majority also expressed confidence in the benefits of technical progress. On the other hand, attitudes toward school were decidedly negative. More than three-fourths expressed disagreement with the statement that "the results of the school examinations are a good test of the real value of the individuals," while more than three-fifths expressed disagreement with the statement that "the school prepares us to live in the actual world."

Although the family remains the strong point of integration, the price of family unity is permissiveness, according to Janne, which makes young people more aware of the authoritative orientation at school. However, the negative evaluation of the schools is moderated by the fact that dissatisfaction is strongest in the highest social classes and weakest in the lowest ones. For the lowest social categories, school is an avenue of upward mobility.

Although the majority of the students indicated that it was interested in politics, opinions were somewhat scattered on whether "our political parties are . . . able to defend our real interests," while only a minority expressed satisfaction with "our parliamentary democratic system."

Thus, two key institutions of society, the educational system and the political system, are not accepted by most young people. In view of the negative attitudes toward schools, the impact of reforms in the French-speaking secondary schools will be of special interest, even though the changes have only been partially accomplished thus far. Like the reforms that have been going on in France, they move in the direction of much less rigid division into streams and greater emphasis on gradually adapting the programs to the students' performance.

A Program for the Future

On the basis of his findings, the author concludes with a set of recommendations relating to education and work of young people in Belgium. Youth needs "deschooling," which means, among other things, the following:

1. Individualization of training

2. Continuous, positive orientation and guidance through an optimal and flexible credit system

3. Alternatives to the classroom system with provision for diversity of age and size of groups

4. Less instruction in learning rooms and more through activities carried out where things happen and where knowledge is increased and skills are developed

5. Alternation of work and studies for the 14-to-15 and 18-to-19 age groups, based on national standards of equitable earnings

6. Recurrent education at all levels provided on the basis of paid educational leaves, by law or collective bargaining, for all types of studies (professional, vocational, and general), for self-improvement, or for community life

Involvement of youth in working life. Youth needs to be involved early and progressively in working life if opportunities for more studies actually become recurrent. This goal requires cooperative schemes involving all the concerned groups and institutions: the learners and workers themselves, the employers, the representative bodies (employer and union organizations), educational authorities, and others.

Elimination of youth unemployment. Regardless of the stage of the business cycle, unemployment of youth must be totally eliminated. Youth must be given the opportunity for suitable studies, work, or paid social services. Whether service should be obligatory or voluntary is a question that has different meanings in different countries, and it is worthwhile to study this question on an international basis.

More self-determination of cultural activities. Real culture is not passive consumption but participation, which means creativity, spontaneity, and sharing of knowledge and experiences. We should expect leisure-time culture to be self-managed by people and not consumed on the basis of commercial "choices," criteria, and behavior. Ministries of culture must take the responsibility for working with representative youth movements to prepare, step by step, for such developments.

Sweden

Youth Unemployment

Sweden has managed to hold down its unemployment rate more successfully than most industrial countries in the 1970s. Although the rate rose somewhat between 1971 and 1973, it fell back and averaged only about 1.6 percent in 1975 and 1976, when other countries had considerably higher unemployment rates. The last several years, however, have been somewhat less successful, with the unemployment rate rising in the latter half of 1977 and running around 2.5 percent in 1978 (see Figure 1.2).

Part of Sweden's success in holding down its unemployment rate is attributable to the fact that, at any given time, the number of persons enrolled in Sweden's extensive labor market programs represents a larger percentage of the labor force than in most other countries. Those enrolled in relief works are counted as employed; those in labor market training are regarded as students, that is, as outside of the labor force. The U.S. Bureau of Labor Statistics (1978, p. 33) has shown that in 1976, when the Swedish unemployment rate was only 1.6 percent, the number of unemployed plus the number of persons in labor market programs (employment and training) amounted to 4.3 percent of the civilian labor force (including those in labor market programs as part of the labor force). Since Sweden expands its labor market programs in recessions, the difference between the unemployment rate and this latter measure tends to be wider in recessions than in more prosperous periods, thus cushioning the rise in the unemployment rate.

Meanwhile, there has been concern over a rising trend in the youth unemployment differential, which was particularly apparent in the early 1970s (Figure 1.4). Even so, by American standards, youth unemployment rates in Sweden are low. The average for 1978 was 8 percent for the 16-to-19 age group and 4 percent for the 20-to-24 group.

As in West Germany and other countries, however, the youth unemployment rate is probably somewhat higher than the official figures indicate. The Swedish labor force surveys show that there is a fringe of "latent job seekers" or "discouraged workers," who indicate that they would be seeking work if they believed that they could find a job. This group is especially large among teen-agers.

Swedish data show the familiar relationship between educational attainment and unemployment in the youthful population. There has been particular concern about high unemployment among the 5 percent of each young cohort that drops out before completing compulsory school or that fails to obtain a school-leaving certificate because of excessive truancy. Not all of these young people experience unemployment, however, some may have left school because they found a job. On the other hand, some of them appear to employment service officers as being impossible to place because of obvious handicaps, such as low IQ, alcoholism and drug addiction, and other manifestations of instability. Another group with particularly high unemployment rates is the children of foreign workers, who frequently lack adequate knowledge of Swedish. Their unemployment rate is about twice that of native Swedish youth.

Occasionally in the 1970s there has been a temporary surplus of university graduates, but these situations have been of short duration. Earlier expectations about easy access to jobs of high status have, however, had to be revised downward.

Youth unemployment has increased in Sweden for reasons similar to those in other countries: (1) the stagnant employment situation in manufacturing; (2) "no dismissal" policies, which usually began as a feature of industrial relations in well-established companies but have more recently been affected by legal requirements, (3) the rapidly increasing supply of women in the labor market (labor force participation rates of women are particularly high), and (4) the rise in wages of young workers, bringing their compensation closer to that of adults.

Labor Market Policies

Sweden is well-known for its extensive program of "active labor market policies," which emphasize retraining the unemployed, moving allowances to help workers move from depressed areas

to areas experiencing rapid economic growth, policies of regional economic development, and countercyclical relief works and
public service employment. Although retraining programs were
originally intended for the unemployed or for married women
desiring to enter the labor force, they were gradually extended
to employed workers whose jobs were threatening to become
obsolete or who were willing to undertake retraining for more
promising occupations.

　　Swedish economists and labor market officials have been
pioneers in arguing that inflation in modern industrial countries
can be held in check through adjustment–promoting labor market policies that are aimed not only at achieving reemployment
of the unemployed but also at preventing or overcoming the
shortages of skilled workers that develop under conditions of
rapid economic growth and that thus feed inflation. Swedish
labor policies are not greatly different from those of other
countries, but they are more comprehensive and involve a larger
percentage of the unemployed and of the total labor force. Expenditures on manpower programs in 1978-79 amounted to
more than 3 percent of the gross national product (GNP) and
are undoubtedly higher than in any other industrial country.
(Table 1.3 shows that in 1975-76 these expenditures amounted
to 1.72 percent of the GNP, compared with 0.63 percent, for
example, in the United Kingdom and 0.57 percent in the United
States.)

Training programs. In principle, the training and retraining programs conducted by the Swedish Labor Market Board are not
intended for persons under age 20, whose training and education
are expected to occur within the school system, where subsistence allowances from the government are limited and are much
lower than those provided by the Labor Market Board. Some
exceptions, however, have always been allowed for young persons who started work at an early age or who had children, for
example. As youth unemployment rose in the 1970s, the reasons for exceptions for youth under age 20 were increased, and
in 1977-78, there were about 3,000 training slots for teen-agers,

involving more than twice that many persons in the course of a
year. The number of those aged 20 to 24 enrolled in such programs, however, has tended to be high from the start, rising
from 30 to 43 percent of all trainees between 1969 and 1973-
74. In 1977 and 1978, the total number of persons, regardless
of age, in labor market training had grown to about 80,000
(full-time man–years), after having been about half of this during the earlier years of the 1970s. The sudden growth in 1977
was due to a sharply increased subsidy provided to enterprises
that arranged training programs for their existing employees
rather than laying them off or dismissing them.

Despite the recent growth of subsidized employer training,
most training under the auspices of the Labor Market Board is
conducted at special or temporary centers maintained by the
board, which are sometimes arranged in cooperation with upper
secondary schools, folk high schools, study associations, or employers. Courses are tuition–free, and trainees receive subsistence allowances that must be 10 Kr above any unemployment
benefits for which they might be eligible. Training at a center
typically begins with eight weeks of general theoretical education, but this period is extended if needed, especially in the
case of participants who lack basic education or who left school
long ago. Vocational courses are held continuously throughout
the year, and trainees can be admitted at any time. To encourage this, much of the training is individual and independent,
with the teacher providing guidance rather than conducting a
class.

Changes in vocational counseling. Sweden has long emphasized
vocational counseling and guidance in the school system and in
the labor market administration, but in recent years the service
has expanded considerably. Full–time officers for study and vocational orientation are being employed in all educational institutions, subject to the supervision of the Central Vocational
Guidance Council, in which representatives of the School Board,
the Labor Market Board, the Swedish Association of Municipalities, and parental organizations participate. Vocational counselors are required to have one year of special training and at
least six months of work experience "outside of teaching."

Counseling begins around age 13 and is supplemented by practical work orientation, along the lines advocated by proponents of "career education" in the United States. In the eighth grade, about a week is allocated for group visits to factories and offices, while in the ninth (the last) grade of compulsory school, pupils spend two weeks in various places of work. Starting in the fall of 1977, pupils in the ninth grade were to be doing much more actual work in various enterprises—from 6 to 10 weeks in 60 pilot municipalities.

Reminiscent of the debate in Great Britain over whether manpower allowances will lure young people away from school prematurely is a debate in Sweden about whether counselors should try to steer young people toward further study immediately after compulsory school or should help in developing a recurrent education pattern. If those who seek work after compulsory school have difficulty getting jobs, the employment service and vocational counselors help them to return to school even in the midst of a term. Thus, by encouraging certain courses to start continuously throughout the year, the secondary schools are encouraging a return to school.

Trainee positions. Apprenticeship has not been as important in Sweden as in West Germany and certain other countries, such as Austria, Denmark, and Switzerland, but the rise in youth unemployment has led to much discussion of the need to expand the number of trainee positions. This has been an issue for debate within the Employment Commission, established by the government to study the medium–term employment outlook. In September 1977 the commission recommended that great efforts be made to develop an adequate number of trainee positions on a voluntary basis. However, the commission also stated, with employer members opposing, that it was prepared to require employers to provide a certain number of trainee positions if voluntary measures did not work. The laws against dismissals complicate the issue, because employers fear being tied to inexperienced trainees through the law on employment security.

Local community councils. Local planning councils for youth, which have existed in some municipalities, were made obligatory beginning in July 1977 and are being established in all local government areas, that is, in the nearly 300 municipalities throughout the country. The local school authorities are given the responsibility of leading these councils, which also include representatives of the municipal authorities, the employment service, and employer and union organizations. Thus, these councils are similar to those that have been advocated in the United States by the National Manpower Institute, under the leadership of former Secretary of Labor Willard Wirtz, which have been started in some communities on a voluntary basis. The same law gave the schools, in cooperation with these planning councils, the responsibility for following, advising, and guiding all young people for two years after the end of compulsory school.

Employer subsidies. In addition to the training subsidies for existing employees already mentioned, employers receive special subsidies for hiring and training teen-agers. The subsidy was raised from 10 to 15 Kr in November 1977 and is paid for six months. The young persons are paid at rates provided for in collective agreements and must be kept on the job for at least three months. Each individual appointment of a young person must be approved by the trade union organization concerned. In practice, a majority of the young people hired under this program are kept on after the six months. In 1976–77 about 8,000 young people were hired under the program.

Relief work.   Relief work has long played a countercyclical role in Sweden, but in 1975–76 the central government subsidy to municipalities for special work relief projects for youth was raised from 50 to 75 percent of payroll costs. As a result, the program expanded considerably.

Intensified labor market services.   In Sweden, employment services for youth are provided through the regular employment service rather than through a separate youth service, but an experiment with an enlarged employment service for youth in 5 cities, later broadened to 19, was undertaken in 1975–76. The local employment offices in these municipalities were given 73 additional officers to carry out the extra work. The program involved not only intensified employment services but also opportunities for training, relief work, and semisheltered or sheltered employment.

One of the significant findings of the experiment was that jobs were available for young people, but they were often of short duration and offered few prospects of promotions. Of course, this is very similar to the American experience, in which the secondary labor market has been found to play an important role in employing inexperienced young people. Another important finding was that very few of the young people refused a job that was offered—contradicting the notion that much youth unemployment may be attributable to choosiness about jobs.

In Sweden, a certain number of young people—perhaps 8 to 10 percent of those registering with the employment service—are particularly difficult to place. They have often tried relief work and have been unable to cope with it; they are on the registers of the social welfare service; they frequently have alcohol or drug problems; they have a history of problems in school and often have not completed compulsory schooling or have done so with very low grades. Joint efforts by the employment service and the social welfare service have suggested that offering these youngsters conventional relief work is insufficient. They also need access to adults who will be available both on and off the job. In addition, both their work and their free-time activities must be meaningful to them. Work is an essential component of the successful treatment of alcohol or drug abuse. One proposal that emerged from the experiment with intensified employment services was to combine a rehabilitation program with relief work. The young person would be able to leave work once a week to meet with his or her group and group leader. In addition, each participant would have a "big brother" at the work place, who would be given modest remuneration. Some small experiments of these types are being carried out.

Issues in Swedish Education

Egalitarian reforms of the educational system have proceeded farther in Sweden than in most other countries of Western Europe. Since 1962 there have been no differentiated streams in the compulsory comprehensive schools for all children aged 7 to 16. In addition, grades are not repeated. Pupils needing extra support have access to remedial teaching. A school–leaving certificate entitles all pupils to go on to upper secondary school in principle, but in practice the door is not quite so open. There are 23 different streams in the upper secondary schools, each having a different subject matter orientation, and some of them require completion of a special course in English or mathematics at the senior level of the comprehensive school or later. Moreover, admission to some of the streams is limited by a shortage of places.

Since 1971–72, all pupils also attend a single, integrated type of upper secondary school (formerly there were academic schools *[gymnasien]*, continuation schools, and vocational schools). The percentage completing compulsory school and going on to upper secondary schools is high. In 1972, Sweden ranked behind the United States, Canada, and Japan in enrollment of 16–year–olds (74 percent), but well above other Western European countries (see Figure 1.8). The percentage enrolled drops off in the later teens, but Sweden remains highly ranked.

The upper secondary school aims to give students a uniform starting point for their subsequent educational and vocational activities. Another aim of the merger of the three former schools was to provide students with greater freedom of choice, including changes in midstream. It was also hoped that students would choose the study routes that would suit them best, without being swayed by outmoded ideas of class and status. In addition, a trend exists toward increased theoretical studies in the vocational lines and increased practical content in the theoretical lines. There are three principal areas: humanities and social studies, economics and commerce, and technology and natural sciences. Each of these areas is in turn subdivided. Some of the theoretical lines—especially those leading on to the university—last three to four years, while others last only two. In addition, there are some 450 special vocationally oriented courses that are not part of any regular program and that can last from a few weeks to several years.

In the autumn of 1976, of the 95,000 students who applied for admission to one or more programs in the upper secondary schools, 78 percent were admitted. In some of the largest programs, such as liberal arts, natural science, social science, and technology, plenty of places were available for students with high grades, few places for students with average grades, and no places for students with low grades.

In the case of vocational programs, the number of places made available is partly based on labor market considerations. The percentages admitted in the fall of 1976 to their choices ranged from 28 percent in nursing to 87 percent in distribution and clerical trades, with 50 percent in motor engineering and 57 percent in electrotechnical trades. These percentages are based on first-choice applications, and most of the remaining applicants were admitted to their second or third choices.

A point under debate is to what extent the rationing of upper secondary school places may lead to diseconomies; that is, savings in the school system may simply call for higher manpower expenditures later on when rejected applicants find themselves unemployed. On the other hand, it is not clear that all of the rejected applicants really want to go on to school. Some may simply be responding to parental pressure.

Although the comprehensive upper secondary schools were partly intended to overcome class distinctions in the types of programs pursued—and, along with this, in entrance to the university—a recent study shows that this goal has not yet been achieved. Decisions to continue in school, as well as the choice of subject in the upper secondary school, are strongly related to the father's education. In fact, the percentages choosing the three- and four-year streams tend to be exactly the same as for those choosing the old *gymnasium* (Reuterberg, 1976, p. 81). Nevertheless, the increased scope of general subjects in the more practical streams has made it easier for large groups to go back to school later and continue their formal education.

Sweden has taken another major step toward a more open and egalitarian educational system through recent reforms in its higher education system, largely based on the recommendations of the 1968 Public Commission on Higher Education (known as U–68). Eligibility for entrance to institutions of higher education has been extended to those who have at least a two–year upper secondary school certificate, as well as to persons who have reached the age of 25 and have had at least four years of work experience provided that they are competent in Swedish and English and have a basic knowledge of the subject to be studied.

The principle of recurrent education was explicitly established in the Parliament decision on higher education reform. Everybody should know, in his or her individual educational planning, that schooling can be resumed without restrictions at any age. Meanwhile, quantitative planning of higher education was to be based on a continual compromise between individual demand and manpower needs. According to modifications adopted by Parliament in 1977, the *numeri clausi* (numerical quotas) were to be limited to certain study lines (for example, medicine) where expansion is relatively costly, while others, mainly the philosophical faculties, were to be open as before, provided the student registered before June 15 for fall admission. According to a new decision by Parliament in the fall of 1978, entrance to all university and college studies is to be subjected to quantitative limits.

When admissions to universities under the new policies went into effect in the fall of 1977, the central administration was overwhelmed by 26,000 applications rather than the expected 14,000. Consequently, those fields of study with limited numbers of student places (those subject to *numerus clausus*) used a lottery system to admit students. This episode apparently enhanced student opposition to the reform. The Stockholm student union (led by conservatives) complained that persons who had relatively low grades in upper secondary school but had points for work experience were displacing recent graduates with high grades. (The lottery worked within each group separately.)

Social and Attitudinal Aspects

The social and political reforms of the last few decades in Sweden have resulted in one of Western Europe's most permissive societies. Among the formal expressions of this are the following: the abolition of physical punishment in schools (1959) and even in the home (1979), the prewar elimination of laws against contraception and the postwar introduction of sex education in schools, the gradual liberalization of abortion laws, and the elimination of restrictions on the purchase of alcohol (1955). The stigma associated with births out of wedlock has totally disappeared, and many marriages are formally unregistered, so that statistics show a spurious increase of illegitimate births to over 30 percent recently, against 10 percent some years ago. Nonauthoritarian principles in education gained acceptance among Swedish parents in the decades before and after World War II.

The most fundamental observation one can make about the behavior of the liberated postwar generations is that they followed their parents' advice to prolong their education. The rapidly expanding facilities for further schooling have been extensively utilized by both teen-agers and people in their early twenties. Participation is also growing in activities promoting intellectual, physical, and vocational advancement. Membership in sports organizations and study circles has continued to grow in recent decades, even though it has long been high by international standards. Manifestations of deviant attitudes have been growing as well, but survey data show that most members of the young generation accept socialization into attitudes and behavior patterns very similar to those of their parents.

On the political level, a youth rebellion at the universities occurred after 1968, when communist groups of various leanings won majorities in some student body elections, but gradually the universities returned to their traditional pattern, that is, being strongholds for conservative ideologies. In view of the social background of most students, this indicates allegiance to their parents' views. Moreover, both left-leaning and right-leaning students have opposed the university reforms, which have mainly been sponsored by the political parties based on workers and farmers.

Young workers also follow in their parents' footsteps in their allegiance to trade unions and political organizations, although rapid urbanization has meant membership difficulties for the latter. With adherence to trade unions becoming more a habit and administrative arrangement than an expression of militancy in a class struggle, it is natural that the young display a growing passivity toward unions. The increase in absenteeism, especially among young workers, may reflect the general decline of authority in society and in the family, but it may also reflect the fact that, as result of increased real income, people can afford to take liberties.

In the schools, particularly in the upper grades of compulsory schools (13- to 16-year-olds), teachers complain about growing discipline problems. There is no consensus on the reasons, apart from obvious factors like the natural revolt against being kept in a status of prolonged dependency while the age of puberty has decreased because of improved living conditions. In addition, the economically and administratively increased access to alcohol, even for the young, must have its effects. In addition, some blame the comprehensive school system itself, while others feel that the need for more individualized teaching has not been met by adequate resources, retraining of teachers, or adjustment of curricula. Efforts to improve the situation by making schools more interesting and relevant are under way through a reorganization of nonacademic activities. School life, it is thought, should be less isolated from the community and from the world of work and should include not only academic teaching but also leisure-time activities. Opening school gates to representatives of voluntary organizations, business firms, and trade unions is part of the plan. Relatively successful experiments in giving pupils more responsibility—both for the methods of teaching and the maintenance of good order—are under way. Developments in these directions, decided by Parliament in 1977, are held back somewhat by resistance from teachers, some of whom are reluctant to take on new tasks.

At the pathological fringe, alienation among a minority of youth is clearly expressed in increased juvenile delinquency, alcoholism, and drug addiction. The "liquor question" has always played a role in Swedish politics, and the consumption of alcoholic beverages in Sweden has been kept lower than in most in-

dustrialized countries. This is still the case, but the use of alcohol has increased sharply among the young ever since the
cessation of alcohol rationing in 1955. Clearly the trebling of
juvenile delinquency since the early 1950s is closely related to
an increase in liquor consumption and—to a much lesser extent—
drug use among the young. Changes in juvenile delinquency rates
are difficult to determine, since all figures are strongly influenced by changes in legislation and in police practice. The new
bulge of young people expected in the next 10 years, however,
will certainly create increased headaches not only for school
administrators but also for the police and the alcohol clinics.

In Sweden, as in other countries, the debate is intense between those who support more police and greater punishment
and those who support greater emphasis on reeducation and re-
socialization. The demand for more police power has been met
to some extent but, on the whole, Sweden can be expected to
continue its policy of antiauthoritarian and prodemocratic education in homes, schools, and preschool institutions, as well as
of democratization of life in work places.

Conclusions

Under the long-established leadership of the Social Democrats,
Sweden has made steady progress toward a particularly comprehensive set of manpower programs and an egalitarian educational system. Whether this development will continue if the Social
Democrats fail to regain the power that they lost in 1976 remains to be seen.

Perhaps the most interesting aspect of the Swedish experience is that, despite the strong emphasis on egalitarian policies
and despite remarkable progress in raising the general level of
educational attainment, socioeconomic status continues to be a
crucial determinant of a young person's progress in the school
system. In this respect, Sweden's experience is not appreciably
different from that of many other industrial countries for which
comparable data have been developed, including the countries
of Eastern Europe. Yet this situation is particularly striking in
Sweden because of the country's well-known emphasis on policies to reduce class differences. How much difference the new

university admissions policies will make remains to be seen, but they are clearly aimed at making the return to school easier for those with limited educational attainment.

Clearly, manpower requirements play a somewhat more explicit role in planning the educational capacity in Sweden than in most other Western industrial countries, although probably less so than in France, and almost certainly less so than in Eastern Europe. The role of an adverse labor market situation in particular occupations in restricting admissions to vocational programs in the upper secondary schools is especially interesting in this respect. These policies seem short-sighted. Perhaps with the emphasis on vocational guidance, students will be counseled to seek admission to other programs with more favorable prospects. The increasing emphasis on work experience in the later stages of compulsory schooling may contribute toward the same end.

Denmark

Youth Unemployment

The pattern of youth unemployment in Denmark is similar to that in other countries of Western Europe; also as in many other countries, the steps taken have reflected the view that the problem will be temporary. Now attitudes are changing, and economic difficulties are generally expected to continue, with no easy solutions to the employment problem.

In Denmark, one of the reasons for the larger share of unemployment among young people is the tendency for employers to take into account the family position of the employee when considering layoffs. Those who have families to care for are kept on at the expense of younger workers who have no families. Younger workers also suffer from lack of seniority when layoffs occur.

Most of the youthful employed, as in other countries, have limited educational attainment. Experience has also shown that young people who have left school early are difficult to motivate for education later in life; thus, the youth unemployment problem clearly cannot be solved by extending the school-leaving age or by offering continued educational training.

In line with the view that the unemployment situation is temporary, youth unemployment has been combated by keeping young people off the labor market until society can employ them. Most young people who take part in courses or enroll at a folk high school must sign a paper indicating that they are willing to interrupt the education if they are offered work. Moreover, according to statistics, the number of young persons that have participated in the various activities that have been arranged for the unemployed is only a small fraction of the total number of unemployed youth.

The view that the unemployed, whether young or old, are not very keen on getting jobs and are content to receive unemployment benefits rather than to accept offers of employment is often heard in Denmark. There is no real substance to this argument. On the contrary, the predominant view among the unemployed is that work is worthwhile and unemployment is an evil.

Some Danish Experiments

Denmark has carried out some experiments of particular interest. They involve both work and education, and have succeeded in creating motivation and interest among youth on a scale hitherto unknown.

Aabæk Continuation School. Located in the southern part of Jutland, near Aabenraa, the Aabæk Continuation School has been so successful that more than 800 people are on a waiting list for admission. The campus is an old farm and is quite primitive. The students and teachers do all the necessary work connected with housekeeping and with all of the other functions carried on at the school, including farming, fishing, repairing furniture, building boats, and repairing automobiles.

The training received by the students is closely associated with the practical work. Creating interest in education is quite easy when the education is directly motivated by work experience. The guiding principle is that the students must produce things that are necessary for survival. Such action from necessity creates quite a different atmosphere from that at a school where the student follows a uniform curriculum. The young people work in groups, and each is responsible to the group; in turn, the groups are responsible to each other and to the school as a unit. Many of these youngsters, who have been quite incapable of adapting to a regular school, flourish here, and the contact between the school and the community greatly helps the students to be placed in jobs in the neighborhood.

Tvind. Located about 200 kilometers north of Aabenraa, a group of schools in Tvind occupies a large campus. Included are a continuation school for those between the ages of 14 and 18, a "traveling folk high school," and a teacher–training college. In all, the schools enroll about 1,000 students. Associated with this campus are schools in other locations that have the same type of program. As at Aabæk, the curriculum involves a combination of practical and theoretical work, and the types of occupational activities are very similar. In addition, instruction is offered in Danish, English, German, arithmetic, physics, and other subjects.

The "traveling folk high school" is a unique experiment. Starting with one bus, the experiment has expanded, and the school now has about 70 buses. Groups of students travel all over the world—to Africa, Asia, and South America. The objective is to gather first–hand impressions and to acquire knowledge of each area by staying among the native residents.

The third part of the campus is the teacher–training college, where training differs sharply from that at the usual teacher–training college. The program requires actual work experience for several years, along with visits to offices and factories. Only after this experience do the students prepare for the final examination, which resembles that in normal teacher training.

The Tvind experiment has aroused great interest and has had impressive results. In fact, some of its accomplishments have been unusual, such as the construction of the largest windmill in the world and building houses without using trained people.

Obstacles to Experiments

Although the experiments described above have been successful, their widespread application is hampered by lack of support from the central government and local authorities and by restrictive rules and regulations. For example, existing laws allow funding for educational materials, but they must be of a traditional kind, such as books and paper; they cannot include materials used in practical work.

Another serious obstacle, by no means confined to Denmark, is that experimental schools are not allowed to engage in production, lest they compete with existing industrial activities. The experiments that have engaged in production have done so on a limited scale in order to finance the project through the sale of the manufactured items. There is opposition not only from private industry because of potential competition but also from public sector employees and their representatives, who fear young people carrying out work in the public sector that would otherwise be carried out by regular public employees.

Problems also arise from the fact that funds available for measures to combat unemployment come from various departments of the central government and from other types of institutions as well. Local boards representing the various administrative departments have been established, but this results in a cumbersome working procedure.

Some Suggestions for the Future

One of the possible objections to these experiments is that they are residential institutions. Thus, only a limited number of young people can participate, because most young people want to stay in their own communities. Accordingly, there are proposals for centers that would be established all over the country where young people could work while living at home.

An aspect of modern society that works out well for most people, but not for all, according to Petersen, is the spatial organization of retail trade and services. In Denmark, as one approaches a city, one finds retailers selling various kinds of merchandise: camping cars, boats, agricultural machinery, and automobiles. Next one finds a large number of gasoline stations. Then one arrives at the city itself, with its numerous shops offering all sorts of goods.

This arrangement often creates difficulties for elderly and handicapped individuals, who are less mobile. They also have problems arranging for maintenance work that needs to be done. Consequently, putting the unemployed to work by serving these needs seems highly desirable. In addition, the unemployed could work on projects to develop alternative energy sources, to collect materials for recycling, to perform repair services, and the like.

The Danish experiments reveal great talent among young people in dealing with practical problems. Future planning to reduce unemployment must take this into account. The main principle should be the "small is beautiful" idea. Large-scale technology production reduces the need for manpower; we are proposing an intermediate technology developed by the constructive efforts of many people, including the young. Arguments can be raised that this type of development would slow the growth of productivity, but if Denmark were to concentrate on improving the quality of its products while conserving its resources, it could sell these products abroad as well as meet the need to change the course of advanced industrial development.

In this connection, the needs of developing countries are relevant. Undoubtedly, the industrialized world has overemphasized hard technology; economists and others have erred in promoting high-technology means of production in the less developed countries. In many cases, people have ended up leaving their villages and migrating to the cities in the hope of finding work in industry, often in vain. Everyone could benefit from a program in which young skilled workers from industrial countries would go to developing countries and live in the villages, as many in the American Peace Corps have done, working among the people there and showing them how to use intermediate technology. These proposals will need the cooperation of employers and unions. It must be remembered that practical work must go hand in hand with education at the experimental centers.

Above all, concludes the author, we must turn away from many of our traditions and habits. The need to revolutionize our thinking goes far beyond the choice between systems—systems that were developed when conditions were quite different. No system can save us; only a change of attitudes can.

Poland

In certain important respects, Poland has had to adapt its education and manpower policies in the postwar period much as Western countries have. Because birth rates were very high in the years following the war, the number of young people moving through the school system and into the labor force increased dramatically after the mid-1950s. Meanwhile, as in Western countries, aspirations of young people and their parents for increased education rose markedly. Also, a rapidly developing economy in Poland created enough employment opportunities, on the whole, to absorb those entering the labor force (though less so for women than for men).

Yet certain aspects of Polish policies differ, though sometimes more in degree than in kind, from aspects of Western policies. For one thing, like other countries in Eastern Europe, Poland tends to adapt the educational system to manpower plans and requirements more deliberately. For another, channels of entry and reentry to education are kept as open as possible; for example, students who enter vocational schools after completing compulsory education may, under certain circumstances, eventually gain admission to higher education, while those who leave school after completing compulsory education are encouraged to continue their studies through evening classes, educational television, and the like. Nevertheless, the socioeconomic differences in educational attainment are much like those in Western countries, and inferior educational opportunities for many young Poles who live in rural areas pose a serious problem, which is only partially alleviated by recent efforts to improve the situation.

Profile of Polish Youth

Polish youth of the 1970s have higher aspirations toward education and work than their parents did. Other goals that young people express are happiness in family life, advancement in social position, fame, and material prosperity. The order of priority of these goals varies with socioeconomic background and level of education; for example, urban youth are most concerned with family life, while rural youth strive toward material prosperity.

Polish youth and their parents differ most in manners and morals. Polish youth tend to begin sexual relations earlier and to marry younger. Interestingly, however, studies conducted in two large Polish cities in the 1970s indicated that young people have no desire to reform society, in contrast with the revolutionary generation of the 1960s. Though differing in manners and morals from their parents, Polish youth do not disagree with their parents' social goals or values, displaying instead a desire to live a peaceful and happy life in an accepted system of values. This contrast between the attitudes of youth in the 1960s and in the 1970s strongly resembles the contrast observed in Western countries, suggesting that the attitudes and values of young people are affected by influences that sweep across national boundaries, even when economic and political systems differ.

Problems of social pathology in Poland are similar to those in other countries. For younger age groups these problems include truancy, dropping out of school, improper behavior in school, drinking, and criminal offenses. For older youth, social pathology is manifested in indictable offenses, alcoholism and drug addiction, suicide, psychological impairments, sexual deviations, and other forms of dysfunctional behavior. Fortunately, however, the incidence of many of these social problems has been decreasing. The number of court sentences for both 17- to 20-year-olds and 20- to 24-year-olds has decreased consistently since 1960, although to what extent this improvement is attributable to public policies is not clear. However, suicide rates have increased significantly, resulting in numerous studies to determine the cause. Suicide seems to be most commonly related to family conflict and to problems in school.

Education in Poland

The education system established in Poland after World War II was designed to eliminate inequalities of the past by following several principles: being large and flexible enough to provide educational opportunities for all who wish them, being so structured as to permit everyone to continue education to the highest level desired, adapting education to meet the economic needs of the country, and pursuing constant modernization. The result is a national school system that is uniform, free, and universal (through compulsory education, which ends at age 15).

Beyond compulsory education opportunities vary, but they are more readily available for some young people than for others; opportunities are especially inferior for rural youth.

The formal education system. In 1960, virtually all elementary school age children in Poland attended elementary school, but only 85 percent completed it; by 1974, this figure had grown to 90 percent. Among those completing elementary school, the percentage continuing to postcompulsory education has also steadily increased, reaching 94 percent by 1975.

Several paths are open to those who complete compulsory education. They can continue education in a variety of general or vocational schools, enter a vocational training program, get a job while continuing to study part-time, remain dependent on their parents, or enter two-year compulsory military service (applicable to males only).

Among those going on to secondary school, the percentage proceeding to vocational schools has increased dramatically-- from 30 percent in 1960 to 55 percent in 1975—while the percentage going on to general secondary schools fell from 25 to 20 percent during the same period. Enrollment in vocational schools has risen dramatically in response to the growing national need for qualified manpower because of significant economic modernization and growth. The vocational schools tend to be very flexible, allowing courses to be adapted to the needs of both the economy and individual students. The relatively rapid growth of vocational schools, however, has recently been the subject of some controversy, because some critics consider the enrollment in general secondary schools to be inadequate.

To be more explicit, after compulsory education, an individual can continue education in a four-year general secondary school, a four- to five-year vocational secondary school, or a two- to three-year basic vocational school that trains skilled workers. A student who has completed basic vocational school, however, can continue education in either a three-year general secondary school or a three-year vocational secondary school. Those from general and vocational secondary schools who pass the final graduation examination are eligible for admission to all types of institutions of higher education. There are also post-secondary two-year schools that train general secondary school leavers for professional work. About 20 percent of those who enter institutions of higher education come from vocational schools.

About 10 percent of all pupils drop out of secondary school. They either change schools, return to the same school after a time, or never reenter school. Dropping out appears to be related to inadequate or inappropriate recruitment methods and guidance systems, socioeconomic status of family, attractiveness of available trade jobs, and competition with other schools and on-the-job training. Drop-out rates are higher in basic vocational schools than in secondary vocational or general secondary schools and are higher among rural peasant and unskilled-worker families than among students from other socioeconomic strata.

Although enrollment in institutions of higher education has increased markedly, not all students who apply are admitted. The increased "output" from secondary education has not been matched by a corresponding increase in the capacity of institutions of higher education. Only 40 percent of the applicants were able to enter higher education between 1960 and 1975; about one-half of the applicants did not pass the entrance examinations.

One of the ways in which the Polish government has encouraged educational opportunity has been by providing student aid at both the secondary and higher education levels (along with free tuition). In 1975-76, about 10 percent of the students in general secondary schools, 33 percent of those in vocational schools, and 47 percent of those in institutions of higher education received student aid. The higher proportion in vocational than in general secondary schools undoubtedly reflects the lower family income of the vocational students.

Even so, opportunities for secondary education in rural areas are inferior, as already suggested. This problem is serious in a country in which more than 50 percent of the 15- to 19-year-olds live in rural areas. More than 50 percent of vocational school students have to commute from villages to the nearest towns to attend postelementary schools. This is the main reason for dropping out of school. The state provides boarding schools for many students, but the number of student places there is inadequate. The standards of rural schools are also inferior to those of city schools, although efforts are being made to improve the situation.

Educational opportunities for workers. The movement toward expanding educational opportunities in Poland is augmented by a comprehensive system of education programs for working people. These programs are available at elementary, basic vocational, secondary, and higher education levels in evening and correspondence courses. Enrollment in these programs has increased tremendously between 1960 and 1975; the number of young people enrolled in evening schools has increased considerably. Workers are induced to participate in these programs through special incentives, such as additional paid holidays for study, shorter working hours, and free consultation time.

At all levels of education, women have increased both in numbers and in proportion. Relatively more girls than boys enroll in general secondary schools, and in 1974 women exceeded 50 percent of students enrolled in higher education. Traditionally, women have studied economics and the humanities, but this pattern has changed, with more women studying technical and scientific subjects. Women now represent a majority of graduates in professions such as teaching, law, medicine, and economics.

Outside of the formal school system, there are many types of opportunities for vocational education. Industrial enterprises have programs of apprenticeship, on-the-job training, and professional improvement. The military service also provides numerous opportunities for vocational training and education. Soldiers may become certified in driving, in car mechanics, in machine and heavy equipment operations, or in various building trades. Significantly, about 90 percent of soldiers who have not finished elementary education complete it during their military service.

Also of special interest, because it resembles some programs for jobless youth in Western countries, is the Voluntary Labor Corps. Young people enter camps for a specific period of time in which they live and work together, acquiring occupational qualifications while helping in construction work or in harvesting. This program has grown, and in the 1970s some 30,000 youth were enrolled yearly.

The Polish government has also emphasized the role of radio and television in education. The second television channel, established in 1970, devotes over 80 percent of its broadcasting time to education. There are regular programs for teachers, for engineers, for farmers, and for other workers (including a general secondary school program for working people).

Problems and proposals. At the beginning of the 1970s, the government established the Experts' Committee for the Development of a Report on the State of Education in Poland. The committee made a detailed analysis and identified the following weaknesses in the Polish education system:

1. Unequal opportunity of education for youth from lower socioeconomic backgrounds (especially rural youth)
2. Insufficient and inadequate vocational guidance and school orientation programs
3. Poor choice of postcompulsory vocational education by many students
4. Insufficient and inadequate postelementary schools in rural areas
5. High drop-out rates and large numbers of students who require extra years to complete secondary school
6. Too many youths quitting school after basic vocational school
7. Too few rural youth employed in agriculture because of the low standards of agricultural schools.

Changes and adjustments recommended by the committee include the following:

1. Compulsory and universal education for 11 years (until age 18) in comprehensive schools
2. Universal accessibility (for rural as well as urban youth)
3. Curricula that can adjust to national economic needs as well as to individual preferences
4. Extensive education that can compete on a modern international basis

5. Continuous education that can update skills as the economy progresses

6. Emphasis on extracurricular activities that would help youth choose the right occupation in the fourth to eighth forms, and some occupational training for all in the ninth to eleventh forms.

Although the committee recommended compulsory education for 11 years, the government plans call for 10 years of compulsory education by 1980.

Employment of Youth

Between 1960 and 1970, when the baby boom generation was entering the labor force, Polish employment policy had to accommodate an increase in available workers that was twice as large as that of the 1950s. Three primary goals determined specific aspects of employment policy: (1) full employment, with distribution of manpower in accordance with the needs of the national economy; (2) full utilization of the educational attainment and professional qualifications of workers; and (3) constant upgrading and improvement of workers' qualifications. The specific techniques that comprise employment policy in Poland are:

1. Manpower balance—information on demographic changes in manpower resources, including the size, location, training, and work experience of youth cohorts

2. Employment planning—assessment of the distribution of youth, the distribution of jobs, and the logistics of matching the two

3. Vocational guidance—occupational advising for youth and parents regarding available training and jobs as well as instruction about various industries and occupations

4. Labor exchanges—agencies that direct youth (and adult) job seekers to appropriate training and employment

5. Wage policy—incentives to draw workers to occupations in which the demand for workers exceeds the supply

6. Staff policy—measures taken within individual businesses to assess personnel needs and develop appropriate recruitment methods.

In Poland, youth up to the age of 18 are covered by the Child Protection Law. The majority of 15- to 18-year-olds, as we have seen, continue education in various postelementary schools. Those who work are either training in vocational schools for a particular job or occupation, training for an occupation as apprentices, or working in light seasonal or temporary work. Some in this age group sign a contract with a business to train for an occupation, and most of them are working in industry, building, trade and finance, or transportation and communication.

Despite the large percentage of the 15-to-18 age group in postcompulsory education or at work, a number of youth are still out of school and out of work. Efforts to encourage these youth to learn an occupation include information programs in elementary schools, radio, television, and the youth press; contacts with industrial enterprises; and activities of organizations such as the Voluntary Labor Corps.

Youth 18 and over are eligible for full-time jobs, and people in this age group enter full-time employment, go on to higher education, are recruited for military service, or seek additional vocational education or training, frequently signing training contracts with enterprises.

The system under which many graduates of institutions of higher education enter employment is of special interest. To secure these graduates for various branches of the economy and to prevent their employment in positions inappropriate for their training, an act was passed in 1964 regulating their employment. The scheme operates through contracts by which students agree to work in an enterprise for a period of three years. The act applies to most studies except for some of the humanities and the arts. Labor exchange representatives in institutions of higher education establish contacts between prospective graduates and enterprises. As a rule, the demand for graduates is 20 percent higher than the number available, which increases the choices for graduates. Preliminary contracts are signed by students in the last year of studies or in some cases in the preceding year.

Students who do not use this contractual method are directed to work. They are informed about prospective employment three months before completing studies by the labor exchange representative in their institution. Graduates who avoid entering work to which they have been assigned are obliged to return half of the cost of their education, that is, about 30,000 to 45,000 zlotys, as well as the total amount of scholarship funds received (those entering military service, the disabled, or those remaining in the institution for additional training are excepted).

After completing the three years of obligatory work, a graduate can go to any other enterprise, whether or not it is entitled to employ graduates of institutions of higher education. A graduate can also break a contract with the enterprise if the latter does not fulfill the terms of the contract. However, if the graduate breaks the contract without such a breach by the enterprise, the cost of his or her education must be repaid. A similar system of preliminary contracts, which are signed in the last year of study, has been introduced for vocational school graduates.

A problem that appears to be of particular concern in Poland is the failure to adequately match the particular training of graduates of institutions of higher education with the needs of the economy, despite the requirements of the 1964 legislation. However, the legislation is not necessarily at fault in all cases. Often the problem seems to result from individuals choosing studies haphazardly or training for occupations for which they were unsuited. At the beginning of the 1970s, surveys of graduates, including recent graduates and those who had graduated in the mid-1960s, indicated that about 25 percent were in jobs that were incompatible with their fields of studies. Many graduates had difficulties in the transition from school to work. They had imagined their future job to be much better than it actually was in terms of wages and other conditions. Also, the respondents frequently criticized the education system, with some 44 percent complaining of insufficient specialized knowledge or information about the principles of the organization of work.

Conclusion

The Polish case illustrates that the problems of relations between education and work in a socialist society are very similar to those in capitalist societies. Despite the larger role of planning in the former, matching training and employment is difficult, and disparities of opportunity among socioeconomic strata are not easily overcome.

Of particular interest, in the light of reforms that have been either discussed or implemented in Western countries, are the proposals to move toward compulsory comprehensive schools for all students to age 18 and to introduce students to vocational knowledge at a relatively early age. The latter policy is receiving more and more attention in many Western countries, but there is little serious consideration of extending compulsory education beyond age 16. In fact, the growing evidence that many teen-agers are "turned off" by school is undermining the notion that prolongation of schooling is advantageous for everyone.

Japan

Employment Problems of Youth

Among the industrial nations included in the Carnegie Council series, Japan stands out as the only country that does not have a significant youth unemployment problem. In fact, contrary to the usual pattern, in which the least educated young people tend to experience the most severe unemployment, in Japan the primary concern is for college and university graduates, although settling for a job that is not considered appropriate for university graduates is more of a problem than actual unemployment.

The reasons for this unusual situation are many. First, Japan has succeeded in maintaining a low overall unemployment rate in recent years, despite some slowing down in the phenomenal rate of economic growth that the country has maintained through much of the postwar period. Although the unemployment rate has risen slightly since around 1973, it has hovered around 2.0 percent or slightly more in recent years.

Second, the pressure for young people to achieve a high level of education in Japan is intense. Figure 1.8 shows that the percentages of 16- and 17-year-olds in Japan who were enrolled in school around 1970 were almost as high as in the United States and Canada, although the Japanese enrollment rates dropped off comparatively sharply at ages 18 and 19. According to Kato, in the Tokyo metropolitan area in the spring of 1977, some 260,000 young people graduated from junior high school (thus completing compulsory schooling), but less than 1 percent decided to take jobs after graduation. All the others entered senior high school. As a result, employer competition to hire the few junior high school graduates who enter the labor market has become intense. Since the mid-1960s, when the percentage of junior high school graduates going on to senior high rose sharply, employers have referred to junior high school graduate workers as "golden eggs." To hire them, employers send recruiters to small rural junior high schools, where fewer graduates go on to senior high, to persuade the young people to come to their offices and factories. Japanese data show that the demand-to-supply ratio of workers aged 15 has been running around 6 to 1 for young men and almost as high for young women. Undoubtedly significant in this connection is the fact that these youth are usually hired for jobs in manufacturing, whereas senior high graduates are more likely to enter the trade and service sectors, where a higher level of educational attainment is frequently desirable (for example, in banking). There has also been a shortage of workers among 18-year-olds—the usual age of graduation from senior high school—although the ratio of demand to supply is not quite as high as in the case of the 15-year-olds.

As already indicated, the greatest insecurity about employment in recent years has been among college and university graduates. In the past, when fewer than 10 percent of youths were enrolled in universities, there was an implicit, and often explicit, promise that graduates would be given stable managerial jobs in either the public or private sector. By 1975, 31 percent of those entering the labor force were college or university graduates, and it was evident that demand for graduates had not met the increase in supply. In the spring of 1977, approximately a half million young people graduated from colleges and universities, but only 16 percent were fortunate enough to find employment in government offices and large firms. Even graduates of such prestigious national unversities as Tokyo or Kyoto encountered severe competition. Most graduates had to accept jobs that they considered less desirable. Moreover, according to Kato, many graduates do not take jobs simply because they feel that the opportunities offered to them are not appropriate to their education. However, there are some interesting indications of the willingness of graduates to take supposedly unsuitable jobs. A recent survey, for example, indicated that 40 percent of the police force in the Tokyo metropolitan area were university graduates, while a few taxi drivers and waiters have bachelor's degrees.

Furthermore, actual unemployment among 20- to 24-year-olds in Japan does not appear to be a serious problem. In 1975, the unemployment rate for this age group was about 1.5 times the national rate—a considerably lower ratio than that prevailing in most other industrial countries. Relative unemployment rates of those aged 15 to 19 are also low by international standards (see Figures 1.3 and 1.4).

There is also evidence that the larger firms in Japan send out recruitment announcements to only a handful of prestigious universities. In other words, unless they are admitted to one of these few name universities, students have little chance of being considered by the big companies. This intensifies the already high competition for admission to these universities.

The Role of Education in Modern Japan

A decisive factor in the incredibly rapid industrialization of Japan over the past 100 years, according to Kato, has been the consistent emphasis on education. The leaders of Japan after the Meiji Restoration of 1868 recognized the importance of education in building a new nation. Primary school education became compulsory in 1871, and the government also encouraged the establishment of institutions of higher education. In fact, the major targets in the education policy of the Meiji government were to make primary education widely available and to use higher education to develop the talents of a small number of highly competent people. The competition to enter Tokyo Imperial University—the first university to gain prestige—was very severe. Those who were accepted were given full government support and encouragement, and they anticipated a bright future. Moreover, the most important aspect of the promotion of higher learning was the underlying philosophy that evaluation and recruitment of youth was to be based strictly on achievement rather than on social status. A young man, regardless of his family background and social status, could be selected as a prospective member of the country's elite if he demonstrated intellectual excellence. In fact, the policy of evaluating and recruiting youths according to achievement was inherited from the Chinese. Thus, Japan to some extent avoided the elitism that characterized European universities.

The traditions of intellectualism and an egalitarian examination system have been preserved—or at least have survived—throughout the modern history of Japan. The majority of Japanese people still firmly believe that higher education is the only path toward a good job, a stable income, and reputable social status. This belief continues despite the shift to a less favorable job market for graduates.

The competition to be admitted to universities is incredibly intense. During the period when entrance examinations are given (February and March), the mass media calculate the "competition ratio" of each university, and major hotels near the big academic centers are fully booked by applicants. High school graduates who fail the examination commonly wait another year or two and try again. To accommodate those who failed, hundreds of "preparatory schools" are available, and the more eminent ones are very successful.

In fact, competition in education in Japan actually starts in kindergarten. Many parents believe that a good kindergarten prepares for a good primary school, a good primary school prepares for a good junior high school, and so on, up to a good university. Moreover, there are thousands of private "supplementary schools" (known as *juku* in Japanese) for primary and junior high school children. The children finish their regular school around 3:00 P.M. and then attend juku for two or three hours to get supplementary and more advanced curricula. Since junior high school is compulsory, every child is accepted by the local public school. However, hundreds of thousands of parents want their children to be accepted by a prestigious private school, which can be a starting point for successful higher education, which implies, eventually, a successful career. In addition, many families are willing to pay even more money for private tutors at home. In a word, from primary school age on, Japanese children live in an extremely competitive world, and the only and absolute good for them is to be admitted by name universities.

The social implications of the craze for education are diverse and grave. For example, when a Tokyo business executive is transferred to a branch office located in another part of the country, he seldom takes his family with him, simply because such a move is a disadvantage to his children, especially if the children are attending a good school. He moves to his new office alone, rents a small apartment, and comes back to Tokyo by plane on weekends.

Unlike the situation in many other countries, the drop-out rate from senior high schools (generally corresponding to senior high schools in the United States and to upper secondary schools in Western Europe) is extremely low. In 1975, 97.1 percent of those who had entered senior high school three years earlier graduated. In view of the strong Japanese belief in educational achievement, it seems likely that parental pressure against dropping out is largely responsible for this amazingly high retention rate. The drop-out rate is also relatively low at the university level. Among those who entered colleges and universities in 1969, 79.1 percent graduated in 1973, and an additional 8.8 percent graduated in 1974 after studying an extra year.

Educational Adaptations

In order to help meet the adverse employment situation for graduates of institutions of higher education, the School Education Law was amended in 1975 to give official recognition to professional schools as alternatives to postsecondary education and to provide partial government subsidies for such schools. A number of vocationally oriented schools had existed earlier, which were under the jurisdiction of local authorities and which granted certificates indicating attainment of particular skills, but these certificates were not equivalent to the formal diplomas awarded by high schools, colleges, and universities. The new law established requirements for recognition as a professional school, distinguishing between professional high schools, which admitted junior high graduates, and professional schools, which admitted senior high graduates.

This development did not signify a shift in emphasis away from the regular educational system, but rather a shift from a monolithic educational philosophy to a pluralistic view. At the same time, employers now seem to be recruiting a better "manpower mix" of university graduates, high school graduates, and professional school graduates.

The government has also taken steps to improve education in agriculture, as well as to provide various forms of assistance to young farmers. Similar programs exist in forestry and fishing.

Despite the egalitarian tradition in Japanese higher education, students from well-to-do families seem to have an advantage in gaining admission to the national universities. Founded to recruit competent young people regardless of their family backgrounds, these universities have charged low tuition, like the public colleges and universities in the United States. This tradition has been maintained: The tuition fee of the national universities is only $200 a year, which most households in Japan can afford. However, the majority of the students in these institutions are from middle- or upper-middle-class families with annual incomes exceeding $20,000. In such families, each child not only has a private room but also all necessary study aids, including good private tutors. As a result, these young people have an advantage in the competitive entrance examinations, especially for such top universities as Tokyo and Kyoto. Ironically, children from less privileged families, who are more likely to fail the examinations, frequently find themselves going to private universities, where tuition and other expenses are much higher. This is the reverse of the popular image of the situation several decades ago, when the typical national university student was thought to be a brilliant young person from a lower-income family, whereas a private university student was likely to come from a wealthy family.

In response to the rising costs of education, the Japan Scholarship Foundation, a government subsidiary, has been expanding its need-based student aid program. Scholarships for

needy students at the senior high school level range from $150
to $260 a year, while those at the university level range from
$500 to $1,000 a year. These sums by no means meet all expenses. At the university level, some 80 percent of the students
have part-time jobs, known among the students as "arbeit"
from the German word for work, a word that became common
when German was commonly studied. The most desirable jobs
are those as private tutors for children in well-to-do families
who are preparing for university entrance examinations. About
one-fourth of the working students hold such jobs, while most
of the others hold clerical or unskilled jobs during summer vacation.

　　Full-time workers have a variety of opportunities to ad-
vance their education. For example, they may earn either senior
high school or university credits through a public broadcasting
system educational program that is conducted in conjunction
with correspondence courses. It started as a radio program in
1953 and became a television program in 1960. The high school
curriculum, broadcast in the evening and on Sundays, corresponds to that of regular high schools. Obtaining a university
degree through correspondence is difficult, because students
are required to earn at least one-quarter of their credits in residence. Thus, they must be on campus for a period of intense
personal instruction that lasts two or three weeks. Many working young people cannot be released from work to meet this requirement. Moreover, the degree lacks the status of a regular
degree.

　　To provide greater opportunities for adults to achieve a
university education, the Ministry of Education developed plans
for a Broadcasting University, which was originally scheduled to
begin in 1976 but has been postponed until 1979. It is to be an
independent educational institution that utilizes the most sophisticated television technology and offers a degree course last-
ing a minimum of four years. The students will have a much
wider choice of elective subjects than in the traditional universities, and the courses will be interdisciplinary. According to Kato,
the success of the Broadcasting University may contribute not

only to greater equality of opportunity but also to a break-through in the traditional and often stagnant university system in Japan.

Training in Industry

A particularly interesting trend in vocational training in Japan is the establishment and maintenance of training facilities by private industries. By 1975, 365 such institutions were authorized by prefectural governors. An example is Toden Gakuen of Tokyo Electric Power Co., which was authorized in 1959. Because highly specialized skills are needed in the electrical industry, the company decided to have its own training school rather than to recruit senior high school graduates. Each spring about 200 junior high graduates are admitted to this school through a competitive examination, and for three years these young people are full-time students in the equivalent of a regular senior high school. Students live in dormitories, and the school has facilities for sports and other extracurricular activities. In addition to the same courses offered in the regular senior high school curriculum, 50 units of highly technical instruction on generators, transformers, and other aspects of electrical work are given. Part of the attraction of this program, which admits only one out of four applicants, is that tuition fees, dormitory charges, and other expenses are all covered by the company; each student also receives about $40 monthly for incidental expenses. Those who complete the program get a diploma equivalent to that of a senior high school and are given positions in the company as full-time employees. After a minimum of three years' work, those who are given high evaluations by their supervisors can go on to more advanced full-time educational programs, including the study of electrical engineering, economics, applied mathematics, and so on, while receiving a regular salary from the company.

A number of similar programs are operated by private firms, and they are highly regarded by both management and the students. Management views the programs as a reliable source of manpower trained specifically for the company's needs, while the students appreciate the guarantee of a job in a large company and the freedom from worry over tuition fees and other educational expenses, as well as over the highly competitive entrance examinations that regular students face.

Discrimination Against Women

There is substantial discrimination against young women in employment. Employers usually do not want women, especially university graduates, because they often work for only three or four years and then quit when they get married. Both employers and young female employees seem to expect the employment `of women to be temporary and auxiliary to men's work. In fact, certain banking firms and trading companies employ women on the condition that they retire at the age of 30. The attitudes of employers affect the attitudes of female employees, who tend to regard their work as temporary and are thus less motivated than men. On the other hand, the employment of women following the 1974 recession recovered much more promptly than that of men. Apparently employers wanted to hire temporary female workers because they were more flexible and less expensive than full-time male workers.

Despite these problems, the number of independent and professional women working in different sectors has increased, but the status of women in the economy remains in great need of improvement.

Attitudes of Youth and Social Problems

The crowded generation. In his discussion of attitudes and values of young people in Japan, Kato develops the very interesting concept of the "crowded generation." Figure 1.6 shows the birth rate was exceptionally high in Japan in the years immediately after World War II. This baby boom generation was poorly accommodated by society in comparison with succeeding generations. Kato (1979, p. 55) describes the situation as follows:

> In addition, this generation experienced heavy psychological pressures from sheer density: their absolute number was 2.7 million; and they found that their lives were extremely competitive, both in school and

in employment. This age group was destined to feel as if they were permanently packed in a commuter subway at rush hour. Indeed, in the late 1960s, observers commented on the physical overflow of students in the major urban universities. Classrooms were overcrowded, libraries were packed, and campus cafeterias had not nearly enough seats. . . .

The sense of over-crowdedness combined with democratic idealism to lead this generation easily to overall frustration and resentment. The violent campus unrest that took place in Japanese universities in 1968–1970 may have its origin in the demographic, sociopsychological, and ideological characteristics of the students of the day. As a matter of fact, it is noteworthy that without exception, the radical activists, including the internationally notorious "Japan Red Army," who engaged in the bloody massacre at Tel Aviv, belong to this particular age group. The occasional terrorism still taking place in Japan is committed by criminals (or suspects) whose ages range from 29 to 33, the former "radical youth" of 1968. . . . An important point here is that this age group failed to recruit any younger followers. . . . The potential younger followers, in their teens and twenties, are more satisfied with what they are and what they imagine they will be.

Television and peer groups. Although the widely publicized generation gap of the 1960s seems to have become less serious in recent years, mass media affect young people today much more than they did preceding age groups. The average number of hours young people spend watching television has been increasing. As in many other countries, the values transmitted by mass media often conflict with the values taught at home and in school. Consequently, each young person may internalize this conflict, a phenomenon that would create yet another psychological problem for the younger generation.

Also, although surveys indicate that young people and their parents communicate frequently, in times of trouble young people today tend to consult with their close friends rather than with their parents.

Juvenile delinquency. The incidence of juvenile crime and delinquency has varied in recent years, having declined between the late 1960s and 1972 and moved upward from 1972 to 1975. Violent crimes such as burglary and rape have decreased significantly, but theft, especially of automobiles and motorcycles, has increased. Also, female crime and delinquency have become more common in recent years. Even so, juvenile crime and delinquency in Japan are relatively low compared with the situation in other industrial countries.

Attitudes toward work. A recent cross–cultural study shows that Japanese youths are more work oriented than young people in other countries. To the question "What is the ultimate value in your life?" the percentage of the young people in Japan who answered "challenging work" was conspicuously higher than in other industrial societies. In another survey that asked the question "Why is work meaningful to you?" 53 percent of 18–year-old high school graduates answered "self–realization through work," while 37 percent said "income." In other words, members of the younger generation today see work as the means by which they develop themselves rather than the means by which they obtain economic benefit. Young people today are the children of affluence and are great spenders, but the work ethic has not disappeared.

Outlook for the Future

Although making any forecast about Japanese youth is almost impossible, Kato concludes with some interesting observations.

The process of transition from youth to adulthood seems to have become extraordinarily complicated. "Early sophistication" has marked the young people of the past few decades, but many young people do not feel that they are adults yet. Because of the diffusion of higher education, many young people experience prolonged dependency upon their families and other socializing agents. Even at the age of 20, when young people are legal adults, they still find themselves dependent. In the past, when most young people began working in their late teens, their economic independence made them feel like adults.

Regarding the education system, grave problems result from the intense competition to be admitted to the name universities. Yet the official recognition of professional schools has led to their increasing popularity, and many young people find them an attractive alternative. Thus, patterns of participation in higher education may change.

At present, Japanese youth enjoy full employment, but this situation is unlikely to prevail 25 years from now. More social welfare measures must be taken to accommodate the demographics of the future, when society will be dominated by an old and middle-aged population. This situation may mean a greater burden for the generation who are now under 10.

Mexico and South Asia

The problems of transition from school to work in less developed countries are not entirely dissimilar to those of the advanced countries, but they begin at a much earlier age. Instead of leaving school at age 15 or 16, youngsters tend to complete their schooling between ages 12 and 14, and the proportion who drop out of primary school or who never attend at all tends to be shockingly high in the countries included in this series. Sri Lanka is an exception to this pattern.

In the labor market, underemployment, rather than unemployment, tends to be the most serious problem, a situation that reflects in part the predominance of agriculture. In these heavily agricultural societies, many children begin farm work at an early age, but the work is highly seasonal. Rural life is characterized by long periods of idleness or underemployment. Nor are opportunities for young school leavers in cities significantly better. Lacking any specific training, and often even lacking literacy, youthful entrants to the labor force are largely confined to service occupations that tend to be casual, low paid, and dead-end. In Mexico, such persons are considered to be in the "informal market." The sight of young people vigorously competing to sell trinkets or postcards, to shine shoes, or to perform other minor services is familiar to the tourist in less developed countries. Less familiar is the regressive pattern of government educational expenditures, stressed by the authors of these essays, that is associated with heavy subsidization of a higher education system that tends to benefit primarily the higher-income groups.

Complicating the efforts of governments to overcome these problems is the widespread poverty and rapid population growth. The problem of improving educational and employment opportunities for young people cannot be separated from the far larger problems of accelerating economic growth and slowing population increases.

Mexico

Between 1940 and 1970, Mexico's economy grew dramatically; however, inflation in the 1970s and financial crisis in 1976 have set Mexico back in terms of economic and social goals. The Lopez Portillo administration has promised renewed progress on both fronts, and, of course, recent indications of the wealth of Mexican oil resources suggest a more rapid rate of development in the future.

Nearly 40 percent of Mexico's population is in the agricultural sector, characterized by low productivity. The resulting emigration to urban areas has glutted urban job markets with uneducated, unskilled workers whose numbers increase faster than the ability of the growing industrial sector to absorb them. Mexico's industry is characterized by a preponderance of small workshops that are minimally productive and that pay very low wages to a very small number of employees. Only 200 companies in 1970 employed more than 750 workers, and although the number of large companies is growing, their labor-saving technology prevents them from alleviating unemployment.

The overall unemployment rate in Mexico in 1969 was relatively low (3.8 percent of the labor force). Unemployment rates tend to be higher in the cities than in the rural areas, and, within the cities, unemployment rates are much higher for teen-agers than for adults. In the spring of 1974, for example, the unemployment rate of young people aged 12 to 19 in Mexico City was 18.3 percent, compared with 6.9 percent for all workers aged 12 years or more. Moreover, the underemployed population—including those who work only part of the year, underpaid workers, and those engaged in the informal labor market (odd jobs, street vending, and so forth)—is vast, averaging around 50 percent of the labor force in large cities. Interestingly, surveys show that the situation tends to be similar in large cities throughout Latin America, not just in Mexico. Moreover, these same studies indicate that 70 to 80 percent of those who migrate from the countryside to the cities swell the ranks of the informal labor market sector.

Although the law requires young people to be educated until the age of 15, many youths begin work at age 12 because their families simply cannot survive without the additional income. Indeed, the proportion who actually continue in school to age 12 has not been large. On the average, from 1959 to 1974, 77 percent of the relevant age group failed to complete primary education, and 88 percent failed to complete secondary school. Yet this average masks substantial change over the period. The enrollment rate of those aged 12 to 19, for example, rose from 23 percent in 1959 to 57 percent in 1975. Over this same period, on the average, about 3.5 percent of the relevant age group was enrolled in higher education, and only 0.8 percent graduated from institutions of higher education.

The national averages conceal substantial differences among regions. In general, the southern parts of the country tend to be less developed and more impoverished than the central and northern areas, with correspondingly lower school enrollments.

Many young people who are able to stay in school must also work. Not surprisingly, the great majority of these working students come from lower-income families. Despite the difficulty of maintaining a job and keeping up with studies, the combination of work and study in Mexico is considered quite successful for university students, because students try to find jobs related to their area of study. In fact, many find positions after graduation in the same establishment where they worked as students.

Although there is an upward trend in educational attainment, the situation continues to be discouraging. There are still 3.1 million youths between 10 and 20 who have received no education at all, and this figure does not include those who drop out at all levels of education for economic reasons. However, there are signs that Mexican youths recognize the need for more education, and some positive trends have emerged. Half of the students in the 15-to-19 age group are enrolled in primary school, some of them in vocational training. In addition, the number of youths with more education than their parents greatly exceeds the number with less education.

Unfortunately, a negative trend counteracts these advances: Educational qualifications for work are getting increasingly more restrictive. In an employers' market, the employers can impose high (sometimes irrelevant) educational requirements and choose the best educated and most experienced people; the less educated who remain, many of them youths, are left unemployed. Thus, although educational attainments of young people have increased, employment opportunities for educated young people are not promising.

In spite of economic progress, inequality in the distribution of income in Mexico has tended to increase in recent decades. Disparities between the countryside and the city are enormous. In rural areas, for example, only about 9 percent of the age group attends the sixth grade, compared with 63 percent in urban areas. Despite the official support of egalitarian policies, a larger percentage of the gross national product (GNP) is spent on education for children from higher-income families than for those from poor families. This fact is at least partly explained by the high expenditures per student in higher education, in which a large proportion of students comes from higher-income families. It also reflects the larger expenditures per pupil in urban compared with rural schools.

Job-training programs for youths, a recent development in Mexico, take several forms: adult schools, teaching "brigades," mobile rural classrooms, and others. Yet those who have the greatest need for such programs do not seem to take advantage of them. Another boon to the youth employment situation, in the view of these authors, would be industrial training programs offered by employers to both their employees and to potential young employees who are now unemployed. Whether the industrial sector would be willing to make this social gesture, however, remains to be seen.

Large-scale structural reform cannot be carried out in less than 10 to 15 years, conclude the authors. The only solution for

Mexican youths at present is to get more education, and few can afford it. From the government's point of view, a legislated shift to labor-intensive industry is unlikely because of the profitability of industries as they already exist. A short-range alternative is to provide the capital for as many jobs as possible in order to close the gap between labor supply and demand. In addition, a minimum working age of 15 should be imposed. This would reduce the size of the labor force and allow youths to become better prepared for gainful employment. Such a policy, of course, would be expensive and require government subsidies, but would be worth it.

Because of the complexity of the youth unemployment problem, however, no substantial improvement is expected for at least 10 years. Structural changes are required, which cannot be accomplished overnight. Youth employment problems are grave and will continue to be serious, according to even the most optimistic observers, for some time to come.

South Asia

South Asia—including Bangladesh (formerly East Pakistan), India, Pakistan, and Sri Lanka (formerly Ceylon)—accounts for over one-third of the total population of the nonsocialist Third World. The combined population of the four countries was estimated at 771 million in 1975. India accounts for the largest share, with about 610 million; Bangladesh has 79 million; Pakistan, 69 million; and Sri Lanka, slightly less than 14 million. These countries also contain the world's largest concentration of poverty, with per capita income in 1975 ranging from $110 (U.S. dollars) in Bangladesh to $150 in India and Sri Lanka. The population in the 15-to-24 age group in 1975 accounted for about 20 percent of the total population.

Youth and employment. Conventional estimates of labor force participation and of employment and unemployment can be misleading when applied to South Asian economies, which are dominated by peasant agriculture. For both subsistence-level farming and unorganized urban labor, the time devoted to work and leisure is not clearly differentiated, and the activities of the household merge with those of the farm or other unit of production. Conventional measures also systematically underestimate the rate of unemployment and underemployment, particularly among youths, because they leave out young people seeking work for the first time, those discouraged from doing so by employment prospects, and boys and girls engaged in nonwage family subsistence activities.

A clear picture of the employment status of youths is not available. The data that are available show a higher incidence of unemployment among youths than among adults. One recent estimate in India indicates that the unemployment rate among youths in the 18-to-24 age group is about 25 percent. In Sri Lanka 37 percent of the youth population was estimated to be unemployed in a 1969-70 survey. These percentages do not signify the real dimensions of the employment situation of young people, which can only be properly interpreted by distinguishing between urban and rural youth and between the more educated and less educated groups. Most of the educated youths reside in the cities and most of the illiterates reside in rural areas, while an overwhelming majority of all youths live in rural areas.

In the three large countries, a large majority of young people in the labor force are illiterate or semiliterate, live in rural areas, and do their best to eke out a living from agriculture and other rural occupations. A relatively small minority with a considerable spread in educational attainment is employed in urban economic activities, and their occupational goals and life aspirations are tied to nonrural, modern economic activities. This picture also describes Sri Lanka, except that almost all of the rural youth in Sri Lanka are literate.

RURAL YOUTHS. In rural areas only families with access to adequate cultivable land can be assured of gainful employment for their working-age members. Others have to compete for the limited nonfarm jobs and farm laborer's work that provide sufficient employment only during short seasonal peaks. A large portion of rural families in South Asia fall into the latter category, and unemployment and underemployment in rural areas are increasing.

The employment problem of young people in these areas is not just the lack of work. When rural youths are not working as field hands, they are taking care of family and household chores, engaged as domestic servants of the landowners, hawking trinkets, carrying loads in the local market, or begging and stealing.

EDUCATED UNEMPLOYED YOUTHS. A large and growing literature discusses the concern over unemployment among educated youths in South Asia—particularly the mismatch between the educational achievement and the expectations of graduates on the one hand and the available employment opportunities in the modern sector of the economy on the other.

Though the total number of unemployed educated persons is relatively small compared with total youth employment, the unemployment rate tends to be higher among the educated than among illiterates and higher at the middle level of education than at the bottom end. It is, of course, a waste of national resources when the skills and knowledge acquired through education are not put to use. Also, national policy makers are especially concerned about the educated unemployed because they are more vocal, articulate, and capable of being organized than educationally and socially underprivileged rural youths.

Indian census data for 1971 provide basic information about the employment situation of postsecondary degree and diploma holders of whom about 13.5 percent were involuntarily unemployed. The highest unemployment rates were in the vocational/technical field, followed in descending order by science, commerce, engineering, and agriculture. The percentage of unemployed among graduates in the arts and humanities was slightly lower than the average for all fields. This suggests that a policy of restricting admissions to the arts and humanities and increasing enrollments in technical and professional subjects— often advocated for alleviating unemployment among the educated—is unlikely to work. The higher rate of female unemployment in all fields is striking, especially because of the small proportion of graduates (less than 20 percent) who are women.

The phenomenon of unemployment among the educated in South Asia is interpreted in various ways, as a result of divergent normative and ideological points of view. Some look upon the problem essentially as a waiting period between completion of education and job placement. According to this view, unemployed graduates eventually either find jobs that they desire or they lower their sights and accept what is available. The remedy lies in measures that would reduce the waiting period and hasten the adjustment between both the number and expectations of job seekers and the number of jobs. The basic tools would be changes in the operation of the market mechanism—restricting the expansion of higher education and improving the flexibility of the labor market so that wages respond to the supply of labor.

Another, more sociological view of unemployment among the educated emphasizes the educational process itself and its effect on the students. People with this view argue that the attitudes and expectations created by the educational system and the knowledge and competence imparted by it fail to prepare students adequately for available work opportunities. These people advocate curricular reform toward a more "practical bias" in the school system, a prominent role for nonformal education, and easier access to education. These two views are not mutually exclusive, and policy proposals tend to combine elements of both.

However, a third view is that the problem of unemployment among the educated is a symptom of more fundamental problems in the overall socioeconomic structure. Holders of this view stress such problems as a production technology that perpetuates waste of human resources and dependence on industrial countries, the persistence of dual economies with sharp contrasts between urban and rural areas and modern and traditional sectors of the economy, and a political power structure that, for example, grants subsidies to unemployable university students but denies basic education to the masses. Yet, recognizing the resistence and obstacles to far–reaching changes, the more pragmatic structuralists will settle, at least temporarily, for measures that bring about certain changes in the structure of the educational system and the labor market.

Educational deficiencies. As already suggested, educational deficiencies in South Asia are glaring. In India and Pakistan only a quarter of those who enter the first grade complete the fifth grade; in Bangladesh, a fifth. In Sri Lanka, however, where near universal enrollment was achieved at the primary level almost two decades ago (through a combination of the Buddhist tradition of respect and support for education at the community level, early missionary efforts, and a high level of government commitment to public services), the survival ratio is close to one-half.

All four countries divide secondary education into two cycles, the first cycle ending at the end of tenth grade. The progression rate from the first cycle to the second cycle is low. In the three large countries of the region, over 90 percent of the population in the 15-to-24 age group is not enrolled in educational institutions; over 50 percent of the youths are illiterate; 10 to 15 percent have a certain amount of secondary education; and the remainder have complete or incomplete primary education. In Sri Lanka, the literacy level of the youth population is around 90 percent, while nearly 50 percent has had some lower secondary education and about 14 percent has reached the eleventh grade or above.

The influence of socioeconomic factors on access to educational opportunities is often underrated. Available evidence indicates that nonattendance and dropping out at the primary level are due mainly to economic reasons. Secondary education is still very largely urban, and boys still make up the vast majority of secondary students.

The poorer groups receive disproportionately less of the benefits of public subsidies at each level of education, because the higher the level of education, the higher the average income of the student's family and the higher the rate of government subsidization. Thus, the situation in South Asia resembles that in Mexico.

All of the large countries attach high importance to achieving universal higher education, but their plans imply a linear expansion of existing patterns. Primary education is regarded as a full-time, age-specific, sequentially graded activity based on a standard national syllabus.

The basic economic factors for dropping out of primary education cannot be altered by any educational measure, but the "opportunity cost" of attending primary schools for the children of poor families could be reduced by introducing a part-time, variable-duration, flexible timetable. (The opportunity cost is the loss of benefits that these children would bring to the family if engaged in some kind of work.)

The countries of the region recognize the need for literacy programs and adult education. Both India and Pakistan have literacy programs for adults, but so far the programs cover only a small fraction of the potential clientele.

Proposals for reforming the secondary schools have tended to emphasize a more vocationally oriented education. Although there is a case for introducing work orientation elements into both primary and secondary schools, the case for occupational training and supplying labor market needs is much weaker. Some schools have included technical and vocational subjects in the curriculum, and most of the students who enter these schools have only one purpose in mind—to qualify for the university. As a result, few students take up streams like fine arts and agriculture, or even the technical stream.

There are a few secondary-level technical and vocational training programs that are successful, but their effectiveness is positively related to the degree to which they shed the trappings of formal institutional training. One such program, run by the Ministry of Labour in Sri Lanka, has over 100 mobile units traveling throughout the country. Over two dozen crafts and skills are taught by this program in courses ranging in length from six to nine months.

Due to the problem of unemployment among university graduates, there have been many proposals for restricting entry into higher education or reducing enrollment indirectly by cutting the public subsidy and making the students pay the full cost. However, some people object that this approach would make access even more difficult for low-income students. Whatever the pros and cons of restricting higher education, politically it has proved impossible even to slow down the growth of higher education in the region.

Development plans for higher education include proposals for qualitative improvement, such as improved facilities, laboratories, and libraries and lower teacher-student ratios. No plans exist for any major structural changes, such as part-time and recurrent courses, flexible entry requirements and prerequisites, credit for practical experience, variable duration and timetable of courses, breaking the interdisciplinary boundaries, and so on. In technical education, however, more part-time and informal education programs have been proposed.

Manpower policies. Although there are a few training programs for out-of-school youths in South Asia, the total number of youths served by these programs is insignificant. The evidence indicates that training programs may be effective in spurring employment and higher earnings when they are accompanied by various related support services (such as credit, management advice, marketing, design, supply of raw materials, and so on), and when they are made an integral part of a broader development strategy of an area.

There have also been some limited experiments with youth service programs. It is thought that, if well organized and properly executed, they can to a certain extent meet their objectives of enriching the students' lives, helping the needy, and channeling student energies constructively. But as the Indian experience suggests, logistic and management problems are often insurmountable, especially if the program is initiated and directed by the national government rather than by local groups.

More widespread are rural works programs that are not specifically aimed at youth but that undoubtedly involve young people from poor rural households. The significance of programs creating employment and channeling income directly to the rural underemployed and unemployed is undeniable. However, implementation of these programs is another matter. The Bangladesh program, which was relatively large in the mid-1960s, lost its momentum in subsequent years. The National Planning Commission pointed out in 1974 that the program was hampered by scarcity and price escalation of construction materials, lack of technical personnel, and lack of sufficient support from the local government bodies.

All of the South Asian countries have encouraged small-scale and village industries as a means of creating employment opportunities at low capital cost and bringing the fruits of economic development to rural areas. India has had the largest and most diverse experience in this activity. While the number of people provided with employment by such programs is large, it pales in comparison with India's total labor force of over 200 million. Moreover, low productivity and low cash income still offer less than a living wage to most workers. Another unresolved dilemma is the conflict between the legitimate concern for dispersing small industries to the most backward and economically depressed areas and the need to select locations and enterprises that make for viable projects.

Strategy for the future. In the concluding section of his essay, Ahmed sets forth his own program for improving educational and employment opportunities for the youth of South Asia. The size of the deprived and disadvantaged youth population, and the source of its problems, make these problems the core of important program and policy issues of national development. Marginal adjustments in existing educational programs or in other institutions and special projects to help specific groups of youths will only help a few youths without substantially improving the total situation. In South Asia, as in other parts of the Third World, therefore, there is no alternative to a structuralist solution of the problems faced by youths—an approach that embraces relevant overall national development priorities, goals, and actions that create the appropriate environment and reinforce specific measures and policies having a direct bearing on youths.

EXPANSION OF BASIC GENERAL EDUCATION. The opportunities for basic general education at the primary level can be widened and a larger population ensured a minimum level of educational achievement if the exclusive reliance on the conventional age-specific, full-time primary school is relaxed. A combined formal–nonformal strategy can be adopted that would (1) reduce the opportunity cost of participating in primary education for poor families, (2) involve local communities in enlarging primary education opportunities for their children, and (3) make primary education relevant to rural life and environment.

FUNCTIONAL EDUCATION WITHIN ECONOMIC PROJECTS. Complementing the efforts to expand primary-level basic education focused on children and adolescents, functional literacy and education programs are needed for older youths and adults. These programs, however, need to be planned and implemented as part of the economic improvement projects for the learner groups. Experience in South Asia and in other parts of the Third World indicates that the help of both established voluntary organizations active in rural development and local voluntary groups is vital to implement these programs.

Reform in secondary education. To resolve the conflict in secondary education between the main function of selecting and preparing students for higher education and the unsuccessful efforts to give it a vocational orientation, formal general education should be emphasized, as opposed to vocational training or grooming for the university. Of those who survive high school, some go to work and others to various higher education programs, but the large majority drop out before graduating. The only way the system can be fair to all these groups is to offer all of them a foundation of general cognitive knowledge and intellectual skills and then to let them take their chances in the outside world. The organizational and structural flexibility suggested for primary education must also be introduced at the secondary level on the same grounds of reducing opportunity costs for participants, granting wider access, and mobilizing available resources for education.

The strategy for middle-level vocational/technical training should be to shift the main burden of skill development to employers and to strengthen the indigenous system of skill development in the traditional sector of the economy. A doctrinaire position need not be taken, however, regarding the separation of vocational training and general secondary education. Some programs combine general education and vocational skill development for youths. The key to an effective program appears to be an intensive and fairly prolonged supervised work experience, provided at a low cost in a communal setting.

RECURRENT HIGHER EDUCATION. The most practical and feasible approach toward higher education development requires a two-pronged attack: first, restricting the growth of full-time, specialized, professional higher education through financial measures and, second, introducing structural and organizational changes that contribute to more equal access to both professional and general higher education, wider opportunities for general higher education, improved professional preparation and career choices, and reduced demand for full-time and high-cost specialized higher education.

Postponed entry into higher education is suggested by the International Labor Organization (ILO) employment mission to Sri Lanka and Kenya. If all students are required to spend two or three years in productive work, and if university selection is based on work experience as well as on previous academic achievement and aptitude tests, it is argued, many students will not need a university degree for a satisfying occupational career, and others will have clearer ideas about the type and level of higher education needed for their own future.

Manpower policies must stop accepting existing patterns of employment and use human resources more effectively while removing gross socioeconomic inequities and distributing the rewards of work fairly. Three specific actions are suggested as major ingredients of a positive manpower policy in South Asia.

REDUCTION OF WAGE DIFFERENTIALS. The average wage of top-ranking public service jobs in South Asia is 15 to 20 times higher than that of the lowest ones. In contrast, the differential is around 5:1 in industrialized countries. Reducing wage differentials would decrease the demand for higher education generated by expectations of white-collar professional jobs, help establish the dignity of labor and attract young people to middle-level skills, and make at least a symbolic contribution toward building a more egalitarian society.

SEPARATING DEGREES FROM JOBS. Formal educational qualifications should be systematically deemphasized as the criteria for recruitment in jobs. The public sector bears the major responsibility for placing a high premium on university degrees for recruitment and should take the lead in implementing this proposal.

PARTNERSHIP WITH EMPLOYERS. An important element of the positive manpower approach is close and systematic involvement of employers, in both public and private sectors, in establishing manpower development and utilization policies and programs. Incentives and disincentives through taxes and tax credits, licensing, and other regulatory measures can be used to encourage private sector employers to support skill development programs.

Overall developmental strategy. In South Asia, any real effort to improve the present prospects of youths must first attack rural poverty. It is impossible to meet the basic needs of the people of South Asia by the end of this century without a highly egalitarian economic distribution policy and an economic development pattern that meets the basic needs of the poor and accepts the need for changes in the pattern of production and investment. A number of case studies have shown that the advantages of growth cannot be redistributed without reorganizing the pattern of production and investment first.

There has been surprisingly little systematic effort in South Asia to increase labor intensity in agriculture. The myth that rural labor surplus siphoned off to urban industries is the mainspring of economic development still exists in these countries. Yet the number of farm workers employed per unit of land in Japan and Taiwan is more than twice that in India, and their yields are much higher.

Similarly, modern, capital-intensive, high-technology industries create a relatively small amount of employment, use up large amounts of scarce capital, and often produce goods that do not satisfy the needs of the people. The policy guidelines for industrial development, therefore, should be maximum use of the most abundant production factor, that is, labor.

A development strategy oriented to basic needs in South Asia inevitably requires a genuine commitment to rural development. This calls for allowing each rural area to devise, within the national framework, its own development plan. Rural works projects, small-scale and cottage industries, production/training programs in artisan and craft skills, young farmers' or laborers' cooperatives, and so on, are likely to be more effective if they are parts of a comprehensive, locally managed development plan for a particular rural district.

Within this framework, a number of specific activities might create additional employment openings for young people. For example, youths could be organized into young farmers' brigades for the purpose of collective farming. Along the same lines, organizations could be developed for women and girls that would emphasize ways of improving the economic condition of families, for example, by raising poultry, eggs, and vegetables, sewing clothes for children, and making handicrafts for sale. These organizations could be encouraged to take on other functions regarding health, nutrition, family planning, and so on.

These suggestions are reformist rather than radical, because they implicitly acknowledge the forces of resistance and the need to minimize social and private costs of change. Without these considerations, more drastic and revolutionary solutions could be employed. The task ahead with respect to overall development and the problems of youths are of such magnitude that no less comprehensive a strategy can accomplish meaningful change without unacceptably high social costs.

3

by Martin Trow

Reflections on Youth Problems and Policies in the United States

A review of the variety of problems that afflict youth in different parts of the world[1] suggests that the responses nations make to those problems—indeed, how different societies define their "youth problems"—are shaped by the unique history and political culture of each society. For example, Sweden and Germany share many cultural and institutional similarities. Swedish education was heavily influenced by German models in the nineteenth century, and both have had dynamic and prosperous economies since World War II, with low levels of unemployment in any age grade until quite recently. Nevertheless, the German reliance on apprenticeship as a mode of inducting young people into the work force is not reflected in Sweden, and the three forms of secondary education that characterize West Germany are no longer found in the highly egalitarian Swedish system. And these very large institutional differences swamp other cultural and historical affinities—at least so far as their public remedies for youth problems are concerned.

[1] These comments draw in part on the essays in the Education and Youth Unemployment series sponsored by the Carnegie Council on Policy Studies in Higher Education and digested in chapter 2.

If differences in the national policies for youth are so great between countries with so many affinities, then West European societies and developing nations such as Mexico or Malaysia can hardly be compared. The developing countries are faced with overwhelming problems, related in large part to their very high rates of natural increase, which tend always to defeat reform by throwing young people into the job market faster than jobs can be created. Rapid population growth creates problems for the whole of those societies and not just their youth, who experience the difficulties it causes in the severe shortage of school places even before they come into the job market. What similarities can there be between Mexico, experiencing a growth of 4.5 percent per annum in its youth cohorts during the 1960s and Sweden, with a level or declining birth rate, a very high per capita income, and an enormous welfare state dedicated, it seems, above all to the reduction of visible unemployment through an extraordinary array of governmental programs?

The temptation is to take a bird's-eye view of these problems, to attain a level of abstraction that will allow an observer to see broad similarities among several societies, in their problems and the ways that they cope with those problems. At a sufficiently high altitude one often can see nothing of the earth below except the cloud cover. But it may be possible to make some observations which are true of more than one country at a time even if not of all of them. It may also be possible to identify the central underlying assumptions of commentators on youth abroad, especially by comparison and contrast with conditions in the United States.

European and American Perspectives : A Contrast

In 1976, the Carnegie Council on Policy Studies in Higher Education invited nine knowledgeable observers in Europe, Japan, South Asia, and Mexico to comment on youth education and employment in their respective countries. These commentaries— and I focus particularly on the modern societies of Europe and Japan—sketch "problems of youth" as seen for the most part by governmental agencies or advisors. They see the problems as stemming largely from rising or threatening levels of youth unemployment. They discuss at some length the problems youth have in making the transition from schooling to the labor market, describe in considerable detail the programs and policies that governments are pursuing to facilitate that transition, and then make somewhat scattered references to official statistics on crime, alcoholism, and drug use among youth. In several of the modern societies, especially West Germany, Sweden, and Japan, one has the sense that there are more programs than problems, and, at least to Americans, the level of official concern seems disproportionate.

Nevertheless, while rates of measured unemployment among youth in these advanced societies are relatively low by American standards, they have, for the most part, been rising in recent years.[2] Moreover, the commentators all express anxiety that the traditional processes by which youth have entered into employment after leaving school are not working as well as they formerly did. There is, for example, concern that the demands of industry for relatively unskilled youthful labor are and will continue to be lower than they have been heretofore.

But all this suggests that what constitutes a social problem is itself problematic, and that conditions defined as a problem may vary substantially in different times and places. Social problems are patterns or rates of behavior that some authoritative people or agencies define as a problem; in the present case, since we are talking about public policies as well as youth problems, the authorities are ordinarily agencies of government. The definition of a pattern or rate as a "problem" ordinarily reflects the level of fear or anxiety that it arouses in the society at large, and a will on the part of government to "do something" about the "problem"—to ameliorate it if possible, but at the very least to be *seen* to be trying to ameliorate it. Thus, the way a society defines and reacts to social problems is a product of its cultural

---

[2] For a discussion of these data for the United States and other countries, see chapter 1.

values and political processes more than of the rate or frequency of the behavior in question.

In European countries, where rates of unemployment (and also of delinquency and crime) among youth are generally lower than in the United States, the very high degree of concern, and the panoply of programs and policies designed to meet the "problem" suggest other sources of worry. I suspect three such sources: first, the persistent trauma left by the widespread unemployment of the twenties and thirties; second, the claims of the Eastern "people's democracies" that they have provided at least full employment for their working population; and third, considerable apprehension that the political discontent expressed by university students in the sixties and since might spread among unemployed and working class youth, with grave danger to the survival of democratic societies. The last of these anxieties stems from memories of radical political movements of both the right and the left between the two world wars.

In many of these countries there is also a widespread belief that a modern society can hardly claim to be a welfare state unless it shows concern, through programs and policies, for its youth. In Sweden, for example, we can see how a welfare state self-consciously creates programs more, I suspect, out of its own meliorist and statist dynamics than in response to real or substantial problems of youth. Problems are there, of course, as they are anywhere one wishes to look with a modern perspective. But the responses that nations make to problems reflect both the fears of the society and its readiness to accept the responsibility to respond to a social problem with governmental programs. The relative weight of these two factors varies.

In the United States, the identification of a youth problem is also a function of anxiety and fear. In our time the chief anxieties about youth in the United States include the following:

1. A concern about the high and rising rates of unemployment among all youth, and especially the fear that this might be permanent.

2. Anxiety about the very high figures reported for unemployment among young black men in inner-city slums. This

unemployment is seen as a tragedy in itself, a potential source of crime and delinquency in the short run and of more serious problems in the long run if these rates continue and if these young men become permanently unemployed or employed outside the legal economy.

3. There is a more generalized concern that the traditional institutions of society that have in the past helped youth in their transition to adulthood—the family, schools, churches, and youth groups—are not functioning as well as they have been. Instead, their place has been taken by a powerful youth culture that tends to prolong youthful attitudes of irresponsibility and hedonism which do not help youth to assume adult roles (Coleman and others, 1973; Timpane and others, 1976).

In their references to the youth culture and its presumed effects, European observers show concerns similar to those in the United States. But in many other respects, our problems, concerns, and responses differ sharply. While we can admire, and indeed profit from, a study of the range and variety of programs for youth that other countries have created, especially the programs designed to link schooling to first jobs, we may finally conclude that their problems and circumstances are sufficiently different to make the experience of other countries of limited value to us. While this conclusion may run counter to arguments that advanced industrial societies are becoming more alike, the differences are still sufficiently great that Americans must look largely to their own resources for ways of dealing with what are almost unique problems.

How must our conceptions of youth and youth problems differ from those in other advanced industrial societies if they are to be useful for designing programs and policies?

1. The descriptions of youth problems in Europe tend to treat the population of youth as if it were relatively homogeneous. The authors recognize differences within the population in age, in degree of training and experience in the job market, between young men and women, and sometimes between youth in cities and rural areas. But in general they tend to assume that young people have similar motivations; that they want very

much to be absorbed into the primary labor market, either after secondary school or after completing a postsecondary education; and that programs and policies that are based on this simple calculus of rational self-interest will be successful. Therefore, on one hand, youngsters have to be given appropriate kinds of education, training, and counseling for the occupations that they will be entering, and on the other hand, the economic system itself must be encouraged and helped to provide jobs appropriate to the cohorts coming out of the schools and universities annually. The essays refer to certain "pathologies" of youth—delinquency, alcoholism, drug use, and the like—but these are seen as problems confined to a rather small and atypical segment of the youthful population that call for exceptional treatment, rather than reflecting characteristics and motivations that are much more widely present among youth. One result of this assumption of the psychological homogeneity of youth is that the essays do not disaggregate the population of youth on other than the fairly obvious dimensions of age, formal education, and sex. As I will suggest, our efforts to design effective policies for youth will depend to a great extent on our ability to distinguish among different types of youth and youth problems.

2. With the exception of Japan, other advanced industrial countries do not have systems of mass higher education comparable to that in the United States. Their universities and technical schools enroll 15 or 20 percent rather than nearly half of the age group, as ours do, nor do they serve as wide a variety of functions for the society. Moreover, enrollment in an American college and university is much more compatible with part-time employment, so a large proportion of students enrolled in colleges and universities are in the labor market, and consequently if they are not employed they are counted as unemployed.[3]

[3] For example, in 1975, of the whole population aged 16 to 24 years old, 44 percent were enrolled in schools or colleges. Of those enrolled, 44 percent were in the civilian labor force, and at the time of the survey, 85 percent of those were employed. Of those in this age bracket enrolled in colleges and universities, nearly half were in the labor force, and of those enrolled part-time, about 87 percent were working or seeking work (Young, 1976).

This is not the case in most European countries, where enroll-ment in school or university is an alternative to participation in the labor market.

Indeed, the implications of a system of mass higher educa-tion for youthful employment and unemployment need to be more fully explored. There may be two completely different ways of thinking about programs for youth employment. One is to see these programs as a way to help those young people who are not enrolled in colleges and universities. This, I believe, is how we think of those programs in the United States. The other is to see such programs as an attractive alternative to higher education for young people. This is largely the European view, and is consistent with their relatively small systems of higher education—systems which, on the whole, they are content to leave relatively small. In no Western European country is there currently any great official enthusiasm for the continued growth of higher education (Trow, 1979). This is so for many reasons, including the deep concern of governing elites that large and growing numbers of university graduates will greatly exceed the number of appropriate jobs available, thus laying the basis for an unemployed intelligentsia, which has been a long-standing threat to European societies. Therefore, in countries that want to keep their postsecondary education systems relatively small, offering places for no more than 20 percent of the age grades, the government tries to make its alternative youth programs very attractive, nonstigmatizing and nonpunishing. But if, as in the United States, government encourages everyone to go on to college and to finish as much formal education as possible, it also develops youth programs for "losers," designed to help non-college youth by providing vocational training and employment rather than higher education. This profoundly changes the char-acter of youth employment programs. Contrast the Job Corps and the Neighborhood Youth Corps with the British or Con-tinental programs that offer training on the completion of sec-ondary education. The American programs are designed for young people from poor homes who are not going on to col-lege; the European programs are not for especially disadvantaged youth but for ordinary young people, most of whom in our society would be going on to postsecondary education either full- or part-time. The implications of these differences for the character and success of youth programs in our different societies are profound.

3. Most northern European societies have substantial numbers of "guest workers," foreign workers for whom the society does not ordinarily provide the full range of welfare benefits. This has been called the "accordion labor force," because these workers' contracts are not renewed during times of recession. These guest workers, as observers have noted, in addition to providing a labor force for basic industry, also fill the low-paid service jobs in the secondary labor market[4] that the native labor force, including young people, will no longer take. An important exception in this regard is Great Britain, which has a significant immigrant population of poorly educated and nonwhite people, most of whom hold low-status jobs, but who are citizens and are provided the full range of welfare services, including programs for unemployed youth.

4. In the United States, the weakness of class definitions of what is "acceptable" employment reflects the much weaker connection here than in Europe between formal education and occupation. In Europe formal education tends to disqualify people for many occupations at the same time that it qualifies them for others. In the United States education (with some exceptions) does not disqualify people for jobs; there is less of a sense that certain kinds of work are incompatible with a certain level of education. This is especially true among young people. Looked at another way, there is sharp competition for even modest jobs from all segments of our youthful population. This

---

[4]Clark Kerr, drawing on earlier work by Lloyd Fisher, anticipated the later discussion of "primary" and "secondary" labor markets in his early distinction between "structured" and "structureless" labor markets. The "structureless" markets (which subsequently came to be called "secondary" markets) were characterized by poorly paid, unskilled, labor-intensive work, transitory, impersonal relations between worker and employer, and the absence of a union and its rules. See Kerr (1977); see also section below on the secondary labor market.

also explains why we do not have an unemployed intelligentsia or the sharp discontent among unemployed university graduates that we see, for example, in Germany, France, and Italy. Another consequence of this difference is that people of varying degrees of formal education participate in some of our welfare programs—for example, the food stamp program. The implications for youth programs of the more egalitarian readiness of American youth to compete for jobs across educational and class lines need further consideration.

5. The political culture and structure of the United States differ markedly from those of European countries. These differences affect the kinds of youth policies and programs that can actually be enacted—for example, they shape the kinds of coalitions that can be put together behind a program for youth. Youth programs and policies also vary considerably among the 50 sovereign states. The decentralization of political authority, especially over education, affects the character of our administrative structures for youth programs. Differences also flow from the differences between presidential and parliamentary governments.

6. There is our legacy of slavery and racism. It is not necessary to analyze the nature of race and ethnic relations in America to recognize that the special problems of central city black youth (and, for related reasons, of Puerto Ricans and Chicanos) are probably unmatched in European countries. The effects of colonialism on the experience of West Indians in England, or Algerians in France approximate our situation, but there remain marked differences.

7. The essays prepared for the Carnegie Council series do not discuss the relationship between youth and the secondary labor market except in passing. Governmental agencies seem rather hostile to the secondary labor market, and develop policies to help youth bypass it in their transition from school to a regular permanent work life. This is in marked contrast with conditions in the United States.

8. These essays, again reflecting official doctrine, make no reference to the significance of the "subterranean economy"

that exists in all societies. In part this "hidden economy" includes people engaged in legal occupations that simply are not reported so that taxes or other kinds of regulations can be avoided. In part, the "hidden economy" consists of criminal activity, such as the drug trade or illegal gambling. This may be a more important segment of the American economy than of most European economies.

9. These papers either do not consider the possibility that some youth remain unemployed by choice because they hold values at variance with the official culture, or else the authors see such behavior as sufficiently rare to be lumped with the "youth pathologies" of delinquency and drug use. But such cultural factors in youth unemployment may be a larger element in American youth problems than is ordinarily recognized either here or abroad.

10. The essays prepared for the Carnegie Council series do not seem concerned with the actual administrative and organizational forms that youth programs take, or with the problems that developing these organizational structures may create. That may be because European nations usually have large and well-trained civil services that can readily take on these programs along with the many other functions they perform. Moreover, the size and diversity of the American population, together with its federal form of government, transform quantitative into qualitative problems of administration.

The Secondary Labor Market

On the whole, governmental policy everywhere seems to be aimed at stable, secure, and well-paying jobs for young people either after completion of secondary or vocational education or after a period of study in postsecondary institutions. Discussions of youth in America, as abroad, view young people as in transition to the state of adulthood, an adulthood marked by a successful fulfillment of a variety of social roles in the family, political, social, and economic institutions. In his commentary on the Coleman (PSAC) Report and other reports on youth, Timpane (Timpane and others, 1976, p. 7) observes that "the primary test of this adulthood seems to be socially productive work within the existing social order." In a word, then, public policy is aimed at preparing youth for what the economists call the primary labor market at whatever level of skill and education may be appropriate. Most of the governmental policies and programs described by the authors of the Carnegie Council series are designed toward this end. Such activity includes training both in school and on the job, educational and vocational counseling, and subsidized jobs in industry. The whole range of youth programs is aimed at bringing new workers into jobs in the stable, secure, and regulated sectors of the economy as quickly as possible.

But in fact many young people in Europe and the United States do not enter the primary labor market directly after leaving school, but spend some time in the secondary market, where jobs are characterized by low pay and fringe benefits and little chance for advancement (Doeringer and Piore, 1971, chapter 8). Moreover, quite apart from cyclical or structural reasons, job changing in the secondary market is so prevalent that employment there involves a much higher level of frictional unemployment than in the primary sector. Thus, high levels of turnover and frictional unemployment may be taken as salient characteristics of the secondary market (Doeringer and Piore, 1971, p. 165).

These jobs in low wage and often marginal enterprises and in casual, unstructured work opportunities are the jobs where "workers with employment disadvantages tend to work" (Doeringer and Piore, 1971, p. 165). But they are also the jobs in which youth who may not be otherwise "disadvantaged" find work, in part because of the relatively weak attachment of young people to the labor market and the consequent attractiveness of such jobs to them. Such young people may show little interest in their chances for advancement and little concern about an unattractive work environment. "Thus they tend to be employed in jobs which share many of the characteristics of those available to disadvantaged workers" (Doeringer and Piore, 1971, p. 166). And Doeringer and Piore (p. 167) continue, "This parallel is instructive. It suggests that it is not the existence of secondary employment per se that constitutes the policy problem. It may be quite appropriate for workers for whom the job itself is a secondary aspect of their lives, whose income requirements are limited (as in the case of teenagers without families) or who foresee eventual access to primary employment. It is the permanent and involuntary confinement in the secondary market of workers with family responsibilities that poses the problem for public policy."

This suggests that the focus of youth policies should not be exclusively or even primarily on their transition from school to work (where governments and official spokesmen chiefly center their efforts and attention), but at least as much on the transition from the secondary to the primary labor market, which may occur from 5 to 10 years after young people leave high school.

In the United States, many young people accomplish this transition without government aid. They enter and remain in the secondary market more or less voluntarily, seeing in their weak attachment to the job (and in its weak demands on *them*) a certain freedom—to remain in school or college, to drop in and out of school, or to try out different kinds of jobs and occupations in different parts of the country, and to enjoy the pleasures of the youth culture without responsibilities or deep commitments. At some point, often in their mid-twenties, these people come to want the better pay, the job security, and the opportunities for advancement available in the primary market. They then enter it, often at the same time taking on new family and financial responsibilities that tie them more securely to their primary market jobs, and indeed to specific firms.

Disadvantaged and deprived youth also enter the secondary market for its casualness, its weak job discipline and high turnover, the relative ease of getting and leaving such jobs, and the usefulness of these jobs in establishing eligibility for unemployment insurance and food stamps. Although employment in the secondary market is seen by advantaged youth to be temporary and interspersed with periods of schooling, travel, and the like, for deprived and disadvantaged youth it may not be temporary, but threatens to become permanent, and is more likely to be interspersed and supplemented by hustling and illegal activities than by schooling and travel.

This perhaps accounts for the very different pictures that we can draw of work in the secondary labor market. On one hand, there is the rather benign picture of a loosely structured work culture combined with unemployment compensation, easy access to inexpensive full- or part-time education or training, together with wandering, beer parties, surfing, drugs, and the whole of the youth culture. As Steven Bailey (1976) suggests, after noting how American youth pass their time in many ways besides working, "In the minds of many young people, serious responsibilities will come soon enough and will last a long time . . ." And he asks, only partially ironically, "Does not youth's very resilience make them the age cohort most able to bear the uncertainties and disutilities of a soft labor market?" (p. 169). But he quickly notes that this is a distorted picture of reality for many American youth, and especially for those who cannot assume that their participation in the poor-paying, insecure, and "dead end" jobs of the secondary labor market will be temporary. For them, such work is not merely one aspect of the freedom of late adolescence in America, to be distinguished from and replaced by "real" jobs when they settle into their full adult roles.

The Hidden Economy

Both in the United States and abroad there is another segment of modern economies, another labor market which resembles and indeed overlaps with the secondary labor market, but with some characteristics of special relevance to youth. This is the hidden or subterranean economy—that part of the economy that is "unregulated, untaxed, untracked" (Lewis, 1978, p. 58). Mark Bonham-Carter, the British politician, estimates that 5 percent of the European Common Market's gross national product moves through this economy, outside the constraints and rigidities of guaranteed employment, union contracts, minimum wages, and governmental regulation, as well as taxation.

A similar system flourishes in the United States. Peter Gutmann, an economist at the City University of New York, estimates that this subterranean economy accounts for about 10 percent of our GNP, which he translates into over 8 million jobs. While many of these jobs are held by people who also hold "recorded" jobs, many are held by people who are officially unemployed. A recent report in the *New York Times* (1978) on "unreported work" notes that "it is difficult to estimate how many jobs are involved. The Internal Revenue Service makes no estimate nor does the Bureau of Labor Statistics."[5] Nor is it possible to estimate what proportion of work in this subterranean economy is done by youth, though one would suspect that, as in other parts of the secondary economy, it is disproportionately large.

The hidden economy includes illegal activities such as bookmaking, numbers operations, organized car theft, shoplifting, the drug traffic, and many other forms of mostly nonviolent and often lucrative illegal activities. People who engage in these activities often also hold legal jobs. But some of the activities in the hidden economy—for example, house–painting and other kinds of construction work, various forms of freelancing, and service work of all kinds—are not illicit. Of course, the whole of the hidden economy is illegal in its evasion of taxes, and often in other respects as well. These jobs also go unreported so that their holders can collect unemployment insurance or work for less than the minimum wage, and so that the employers can avoid paying obligatory fringe benefits and taxes.

In northern Europe, Flora Lewis reports, the hidden economy remains a craftsman's domain. In this way, painters, plumbers, electricians, dressmakers, and other kinds of service workers add to their income and provide services otherwise hard to get

[5] Since this article appeared, the IRS has been studying this issue. Its preliminary calculations "point to underground activity worth roughly $100 billion annually, give or take $10 billion. Some $25 billion of that goes into organized crime, the [study] group says" (*Wall Street Journal*, 1978). See also *Fortune* (1978), Freud (1979), Gutmann (1977), *Business Week* (1978).

quickly. In Italy, she notes, the hidden economy is much more pervasive and much more highly organized—a genuine alternative economy. In Europe as a whole, this part of the economy appears to be as much a response to guaranteed employment laws governing the primary economy as to taxes and fringe benefits. For example, in West Germany, Flora Lewis reports, it is calculated that for every half mark an employer grants in a pay increase, he must add 1.8 marks in "social costs" (Lewis, 1978, p. 54). But even there, one suspects that the appeal to youth of the secondary labor market also extends to the hidden parts of the economy. And youth workers may be especially attractive to small underground employers who want to preserve the right to lay workers off in response to market demand, especially in societies where laws make discharge from most regular jobs increasingly difficult or impossible.

In the United States, the illegal economy itself is substantial, especially in inner–city slum areas. This certainly distorts our unemployment statistics for youth (as for adults), and thus affects the policies and programs for youth that are predicated on those data. But far more important, the economy of crime, like the larger hidden economy, is an important alternative both to legal employment, especially in the secondary labor market, and to public youth programs (see Bullock, 1973). In a large and careful study of unemployment in 30 big American cities done in the late 1960s, Stanley Friedlander (1972, p. 113) observed that: "As an alternative to the legitimate dual market, the illegal labor market offers considerable incentive to many residents of slum areas. Crime and hustling can provide higher incomes, more status and prestige, more exciting work, and better hours and working conditions than the low–wage casual sectors. Moreover, this illegal market may be of sufficient size to affect the extent to which, and the ways in which slum residents participate in the regular dual market." He continues, "If the illegal market is large and accessible, if it provides alternative job opportunities to ghetto dwellers, it should have a definite impact on slum unemployment," although its effect on *measured* unemployment is another matter.

Friedlander (1972, p. 113) concludes:

It is not important to obtain a precise estimate of the income received by the residents of slum areas from illegal business activities. What is essential is to recognize that illegal activities supply substantial income to residents of poverty areas, as well as other members of the urban population. The impact and consequences of the illegal money on unemployment and employment, on labor force behavior, and on wage rates, taxation, and manpower and poverty programs are not known and must be examined carefully.

Government programs and policies and the regular legitimate labor market cannot compete effectively with the opportunities offered in the illegal marketplace. It cannot be profitable to pursue economic, educational, and manpower policies that do not recognize the problems and barriers presented by the opportunities in the illegal economy.[6]

Elsewhere in the same volume, Friedlander reports the surprising findings that in the 30 cities he studied, "the cities that had the greatest amount of property crime in 1966 had a significantly lower unemployment rate in the slums. Apparently income-earning potential in the illegal sector offered an acceptable alternative to secondary employment in the slums" (Friedlander, 1972, p. 114).

There has been some discussion in the literature on youth about whether unemployment among youth leads them into delinquency and crime, or whether youngsters who get involved in delinquent activities are as a result more likely to be unemployed, or whether some prior characteristics dispose certain young people both to delinquent and criminal activities on the one hand, and to unemployment on the other. But all of these

[6] Friedlander (1972, p. 113) speculates that adults who are engaged in illegal activities "are likely to tell enumerators that they are employed, lest their standard of living would arouse suspicion." But for youth living with parents this may not be an important consideration, not as important, perhaps, as maintaining eligibility for unemployment insurance, food stamps, and other forms of welfare.

speculations assume a positive correlation between crime and unemployment, although differing about the nature of the cause and connection. Friedlander, in the passage just quoted, reports an inverse relationship between crime rates and unemployment rates. But for a very sharp contrast between American and European circumstances, compare the analysis of von Dohnanyi (1978, pp. 70-75), who explains a similar inverse relationship between unemployment and crime rates among German youth by a quite different set of processes. In Germany, he suggests, unemployed youth feel terribly isolated and outside of respectable society. Rather than engage in delinquent activities, which would push them even further outside respectable society, they become compulsive conformists, and avoid any appearance of being unrespectable. Therefore, the higher the rates of unemployment, the less delinquency these youths engage in. This contrast says worlds about the different assumptions made in Germany and the United States about unemployed youth. In Europe, illegal activity is not seen as an alternative form of employment for youth, but rather as an aberrant activity, a pathology of a relatively small segment of the population. Thus, it is addressed not as an economic activity but as something outside the economic sphere. That is not the case in the United States, where, for example, Friedlander (1972, p. 187) estimates that nearly 40 percent of the sample of residents of Harlem that he studied in 1966 had an income from illegal activities.[7]

It is therefore all the more surprising to find no mention in various official publications on youth and youth unemployment of illegal activities as a significant factor in the employment of youth in our central cities (see, for example, Congressional Budget Office, 1976). It is not clear why illegal activities are not ordinarily taken into account in discussions of youth employment. It may be that, since arrest rates of minority youth run about ten times as high as rates among white youth in big cities, the whole issue of youth crime and illegal activities has become so touchy that public agencies are not able to discuss it or its

[7]Bullock estimates that illegal activities are "probably the greatest single source of market income in the central city" (1973, p. 99).

implications for employment or unemployment freely.[8] But this is a great pity because, as Friedlander (1972) notes without moralizing, illegal employment and its economic and other rewards strongly affect the success of policies and programs designed to help youth in their transition to adult roles.

Cultural Unemployment

The essays in the Carnegie Council series do not discuss the extent or significance of "culturally determined unemployment." By this I mean the readiness of people, specifically young people, to remain unemployed rather than to accept work they consider demeaning and humiliating. The concept of "cultural unemployment" could be more broadly defined to include all attitudes and values that enter into employment patterns other than the rational calculus of gain and loss that characterizes *homo economicus.*

The Carnegie essays do make occasional reference to attitudes and values of youth. For example, several express concern that a great increase in the number of university graduates will lead to an oversupply for occupations traditionally filled by university graduates. On the other hand, they note that the tightening of the special job market for university graduates may discourage some secondary school graduates from entering universities, and thus increase the number of young people entering the labor market directly out of secondary school (see, for example, von Dohnanyi [1978], pp. 88-90). Some essays point to the way in which "guest workers" and their children have taken jobs, especially in the secondary economy, which native youth will not accept any longer, because the jobs are perceived as demeaning and beneath them. But anything that narrows the markets in which youth seek work will, over time and on average, raise the unemployment rate. It may also drive wages in those demeaning jobs up, or create a group of workers who are

[8]It may also be that official agencies tend to rely on "hard" official statistics and are reluctant to introduce issues on which there are few good data, and what few exist are hard to interpret.

stigmatized by association with those jobs. It may also affect the character of the products or services produced by the pariah sector of the economy.

In any event, cultural and normative factors that shape the acceptance of employment deserve more systematic attention than they have received. In the literature on youth, one sees a certain reluctance to discuss these factors, perhaps because they are thought to have a trivial effect on youth behavior in the labor market. Moreover, they cannot be measured easily, certainly not through census type surveys. And, like the illegal economy, cultural unemployment gets analysts and commentators into the murky areas of attitudes, values, and preferences— forces and concepts that make many economists uneasy and governmental agencies even more so.

Because youth is heavily employed in the secondary labor market, we assume that they represent a structural tendency of the market. Some of that participation is surely a product of the preferences of youth for jobs that carry few obligations even as they offer little future. But motivations are hard to ascertain with confidence; we cannot be sure that we can determine motivations by asking people why they do or do not take jobs, since in the very asking we influence their responses.

Nevertheless, some writers do speak about cultural factors in employment. For example, according to a recent study in New York:

> There are hundreds of thousands—(16% of all New Yorkers 18 years old or over) opting to be sustained by public assistance or unemployment compensation rather than taking jobs that do not suit their skills or interests. This growing attitude is more characteristic of the less educationally skilled, the economically disadvantaged minorities and the young—those persons most likely found among the ranks of the unemployed. (Gray and Bolce, 1977, p. 37)

The authors continue:

Causes of the current decline of the work ethic vary by group. Among the disadvantaged several factors appear to play a role.

1. The way our system operates, the material differences between not working and holding a minimum-wage job is small when all the fringe benefits available through public assistance, but not through minimum-wage jobs, are taken into account. This material difference is not always large enough to motivate a person to accept a dead-end job that does not suit him.

2. Not all sub-cultures in our society define working for a living as central to their life orientation. This is particularly so among the lower class and among some women and youth (p. 37).

The authors conclude that "any policy that ignores the trend toward voluntary unemployment will guarantee its own failure. If the Government attacks the unemployment problems through a campaign to create jobs of only minimum desirability (for example, through the Humphrey-Hawkins bill), the outcome will fall short of the policy goals and will probably make matters worse" (p. 37).

In a similar vein, Friedlander (1972) notes that in his large study of urban American unemployment in 30 cities in the end of the 1960s, he found high unemployment rates in the slums even in cities with large service sectors. He explains this finding in the following way: "The civil rights movement and the development of black pride led many young blacks to reject employment in the low wage service sector. Alternative income sources were more readily available, either from the welfare system or from illegal activities" (Friedlander, p. 118).[9]

If we accept that some youth unemployment is voluntary, as it is among adults, then it follows that such people are neither

[9] For accounts of lower-class black subcultures, and of the norms and values held by their members that affect their behaviors in the job market, see Stack (1974) and Liebow (1967).

wholly in or out of the labor market, but "in" or "out" depending on the nature of the jobs available, their status and convenience, as well as their remuneration. But if some significant number of people who are counted as "unemployed" are so at least in part voluntarily, then that certainly affects the meaning we have to attach to the concept "unemployment" and to the "unemployment rates" which result.

But unemployment rates, while seriously flawed as measures of the relation of the "labor force" to the "job market," are nevertheless necessary for the conduct of public business; they are, for example, used in the formulas governing the disbursement of some $17 billion of federal funds to state and local governments (Shiskin, 1978; Shiskin and Stein, 1975). Thus, unemployment rates serve as index numbers, providing a reasonable and legitimate basis for the allocation of federal funds to local authorities. However useful such figures may be for public administration, they do not provide a good basis for designing job and training programs for youth. They do not, for example, tell us how many young people in any given area are, in fact, potential candidates for whatever youth programs the federal government may design for them.[10]

A great variety of cultural and normative factors shape the job market behavior of advantaged as well as disadvantaged and deprived youth. For example, the one major group in the United States which, like European university graduates, still expects a certain kind of job appropriate to their educational achievement, is composed of recipients of doctoral degrees in the humanities and social sciences who have nominally been prepared for positions in the academic professions. Such people resist taking other kinds of jobs. But if I emphasize the importance of these cultural factors in the inner-city areas and among minority groups, it is because these disadvantaged and deprived youth are, by and large, objects of our deepest concerns as of our public policies

[10]The effects of "voluntary unemployment" on the validity of unemployment statistics must be added to the effects of the many other factors which make unemployment statistics (especially for youth) inaccurate and unreliable. See footnote 16.

and programs. As various observers suggest, we can hardly design effective programs unless we take into account the behavior of youth that may work at odds with whatever policies we design.

Types of Youth and Policies for Youth

There is no single "youth" problem that would be responsive to public policy. And that suggests that the broad concept "youth" may be of only limited value. Put another way, when we are thinking of public policies, we are less concerned with similarities among "youth" than with the differences among them. We are especially concerned with differences in behavior among youth that give rise to "social problems," and most especially with differences that are or might be responsive to public intervention. Social scientists and historians may find a broad concept of "youth" useful in exploring changes in the economy, the family, education, and other aspects of social life over the past 200 years that have affected the life and experience of young people in modern industrial societies (see, for example, Gillis, 1974). Others may analyze "youth" as a stage in the life cycle, and discuss the special problems (for example, of psychosexual development) that are experienced by modern youth between the onset of puberty and the assumption of full adult roles (see, for example, Erikson, 1964). But when we turn to the social problems that have been created or exacerbated by these social-historical developments, and to possible interventions by public agencies to deal with those problems or their effects, the concept "youth" is no longer of much use to us. For the problems take very different forms in different parts of our society (and in other societies). Our response must be adapted to the specific forms that problems take, and not to the broad generic difficulties characterizing the whole of the "youth" population. For effective policy (and perhaps for more illuminating analyses as well) we must disaggregate.

What characteristics of "youth" are relevant to the design of policies for them? Certainly there are important and relevant differences between age categories, and by the level of education completed. But over and above those there are two further characteristics of youth that should have a bearing on the design of public policies and programs.

One of these, simply enough, is the financial resources available to the young person, and that means in most cases his family's resources. The issue here is whether those resources are "adequate" to allow a young person to realize his or her potential, that is, to find a place in the world that is roughly commensurate with his or her own talents, energies, and aspirations. From another perspective, for what group or proportion of youths would additional public aid—either through cash transfers, the delivery of services, or the provision of subsidies—make an appreciable difference to their fulfillment of their own potential and to the society at large? For some young people, a lack of funds does not limit their development; for others, lack of resources at this period of their lives is clearly a sharp limitation on what they do and what they can achieve later on. Without begging any questions about the responsibilities of the state in redressing these inequalities, or where and how the lines should be drawn, one dimension of a typology of youth might be defined by the difference between youth for whom family resources are adequate for their preparation and development during these years, and those for whom it is inadequate.

Another characteristic of youth relevant to policies for them is whether their socialization and education up to the ages of 16 to 18 enable them to move toward and then accept and fulfill socially responsible adult roles in the society. While there is less consensus now than formerly on what are acceptable roles and behavior in the family, and in political and religious institutions, most people still believe that a person should be able to gain and hold a job when jobs are available and not be supported either by public welfare or through criminal activities. But even the most undemanding jobs require some motivation and ability to delay gratification, to plan ahead, and to get to work on time more or less regularly. Most jobs in modern society also demand minimum levels of competence in reading, writing, and arithmetic; the capacity to accept a certain measure of

Figure 3.1. A typology of youth

		Early Education and Socialization	
		Adequate	Inadequate
Family Financial Resources	Adequate	The Advantaged	The Alienated
	Inadequate	The Disadvantaged	The Deprived

responsibility; and the ability to enter into and sustain personal relationships. In considering policies for youth, it may be useful to distinguish between young people whose early education and socialization have given them the motivation, skills, and personal qualities that will enable them to get and hold jobs, and those who are markedly deficient in any or all of these respects.

If we consider these two variables or dimensions together, we find that they generate a typology of youth that may have relevance to public policies and programs (Figure 3.1). If for simplicity we simply dichotomize these variables, they produce four categories of youth, each with its own rather different characteristics.

The Advantaged

These young men and women have both the personal and financial resources to move toward adult roles that are roughly commensurate with their talents and ambitions. At first glance it might appear that they do not have any problems that would call for public programs of aid and support. But these are the people upon whom society most heavily depends, and so the quality of the institutions, training, and experience available to this segment of youth is crucial to their development and ultimately to the society which they will be largely sustaining. Society ought to be concerned about the skills and knowledge they will bring to their adult jobs and other roles; it should be concerned also about the fit between the skills gained and expectations engendered in their schooling, and the opportunities they will have to use those skills to fulfill those expectations in their adult careers. No society can neglect the institutions and programs designed for advantaged youth on the grounds that these people can look after themselves—and no society does. In the United States the institution that has the major responsibility for preparing advantaged youth for adult roles is our system of colleges and universities.

The Alienated

These are young people who have not been deprived economically, but who are having difficulty in their transition to adult roles because of other problems relating to their earlier socialization, education, or both. I call them the "alienated" because many are psychologically and emotionally outside the society in which they live; their behavior is governed by their feeling apart from and often hostile to the dominant culture and social institutions. Some of these young people are in fact seeking and creating alternative socializing communities—in communes, in religious sects (Eastern or fundamentalist Christian), or in polical communities that embody distinctive philosophies and life styles. Others seek further education outside the traditional educational system which many in this category have found punishing. Some are simply downwardly mobile for complicated reasons that involve their natural abilities and energies, their aspirations and values, their family dynamics and relationships to their parents, and various combinations of these forces.

The Disadvantaged

In many ways, this group presents the most rewarding, that is, the most soluble, problems for public policy. These young men and women have personal and academic skills, motivations, and in most cases family encouragement. They need financial aid, counseling, and in some cases publicly supported programs of employment to translate their potential into adult achievement. It is this group that provides the "new" students in postsecondary education, and whose members profit most from state scholarship programs and Basic Opportunity Grants, low-cost loans, and inexpensive community and state colleges. Young people in this category are perhaps the best candidates for various kinds of nontraditional education, such as work-study programs. Many need and can use educational and career counseling. Young people in this category also need and put to good use various kinds of publicly supported community activities for youth, such as teams and youth clubs. Such recreation groups also have important functions in providing information and advice about educational and job opportunities.

The Deprived

In this category are to be found the young men and women who have the most severe and difficult problems of growth and maturation, who are at once most in need of help from public and private sources and least able to seek it out or profit from such help when it is offered. For these youth, a combination of poverty, inadequate education, and weak psychological resources results in a litany of human and social disaster: high rates of criminal activity, drug and alcohol addiction, chronic unemployment, physical and mental illness, dependence on public welfare, and institutionalization. Society currently spends large sums on these youth—on the police, the courts, jails and prisons, and systems of probation and parole; on drug abuse programs; and on other forms of support. The real costs of deprivation are infinitely greater: The threat to urban life that lies in the high rates of violent street crime, much of it committed by deprived youth, and the loss to society of their potential contributions, are only the greatest of those hidden costs.

Deprived youth are a source of much of the national anxiety and concern about the problem of youth in general.[11] The problems of deprived youth are the object of many of the public policies and programs for youth, though few of them can be shown to have had much success with this group. This is partly because public agencies have not recognized important differences between disadvantaged and deprived youth. While the former need and can profit from additional resources for gaining skills and entry to adult jobs, deprived youth often have

[11]See, for example, *Newsweek*, 1978, which, like much of the media, equates "black youth" with deprived black youth.

trouble using these resources, whether they be publicly supported job programs or financial aid to enable them to go to college. A combination of personality difficulties (including a low self-image and an inability to postpone gratification), cultural attitudes towards work, and a poor educational background make it difficult for deprived youth to get and hold legitimate jobs or gain educational credentials. In addition, their networks of friends and kin are not able to provide good leads to legitimate jobs or are actually recruiting them to the subterranean economy of "hustling," petty theft, and the like.

Deprived youth may well need more than additional resources; they may need, and at an earlier age than this essay is considering, a different kind of basic socialization, either in their own families or in a residential institution such as a boarding school. Many deprived youth do in fact have experience with "residential institutions" in the form of correctional institutions and reform schools, but those institutions are heavily stigmatized and have the difficult if not impossible task of trying to resocialize their youthful inmates under conditions of compulsion. The problem is further complicated when large numbers of deprived youth live close together, as in our inner cities, and create informal institutions, associations, and a subculture of delinquency. Students of delinquency debate about the nature and strength of these subcultures, and the degree to which they stand opposed to the dominant values of the surrounding society (see, for example, *International Encyclopedia of the Social Sciences,* 1968, pp. 74-96). But the evidence suggests that these subcultures sustain their own attitudes toward work and toward criminal activity of various kinds, and tend also to dominate the overcrowded correctional institutions, canceling or reversing their impact as resocializing agencies.

In any event, the category of deprived youth is itself not homogeneous. Some in this category are not so handicapped that they cannot profit from job programs of the kind represented by the Neighborhood Youth Corps and CETA youth titles. On the whole, however, our impression is that the local agencies that administer federally funded programs are more likely to give the available jobs to disadvantaged rather than to deprived youth.[12] Disadvantaged youth, as contrasted with deprived youth, are more likely to get to work on time, are motivated to get and hold jobs, and are thus attractive to local "subcontractors" of federal programs who want to establish a good "track record" in order to be re-funded in the future. In addition, and especially in the minority communities of our inner cities, these disadvantaged youth are likely to be the sons and daughters of the "respectable" ethnic community members—the people who vote and belong to (or otherwise influence) the ethnic organizations that distribute much of this federal support. The jobs, which constitute the effective patronage that the youth programs provide, are thus distributed among the sons and daughters of the more effective members of the ethnic community and not its outcasts. Here, as in so much of social life, the people who make best use of public services and programs are not those at the very bottom of the social heap, but those one or two steps up who are more able, more motivated, and who use these programs as vehicles for social mobility out of the slums and out of the lower classes. Disadvantaged youth, who often have a network of friends and family, can use that network to gain access to federally supported job programs, which in turn provide additional work experience and connections to a primary labor market. So some youth are able to use the benefits available to them to gain other resources, and in a series of steps progressively move into more rewarding, better paying, more secure adult jobs; others, with perhaps fewer personal and social resources to begin with, are caught in a lifetime of dreary, poorly paid, and insecure secondary labor market jobs; still others are trapped in a cycle of crime and dependency. This pattern defines the problem for public policies for youth.[13]

[12] These remarks are based on studies of CETA–funded youth programs in the San Francisco Bay Area carried out during the summer of 1978 by William Denyer, Pat Hayashi, Dale Shimasaki, Walter Wong, and myself. The work was supported by the Carnegie Council on Policy Studies in Higher Education.

[13] In this paper I have been talking about federally supported youth programs as if their only function were to provide additional resources—

Types of Secondary Labor Market Jobs

Thus, we need to analyze the meanings and functions of the secondary job market for different kinds of youth, and specifically for advantaged, disadvantaged, alienated, and deprived youth. The significance of youthful employment, both for individuals and the larger society, may very well center on how different segments of youth view the transitory and ephemeral job opportunities of the secondary labor market.

But we also need to look more closely at the variety of jobs and work that make up the secondary labor market. At best, some jobs in the secondary market give young people responsibilities, experience in working with other people, experience in getting to work regularly and on time, how to use and care for tools, and other useful skills and habits. Many jobs held by young people in fast-food chains may in fact perform some of these functions. But other kinds of jobs in the secondary labor market teach attitudes and habits that are downright harmful to young peoples' future careers. For example, Doeringer and Piore (1971, p. 175) observe:

> While only low levels of "job skills" are developed in secondary employment, certain modes of behavior and thought are encouraged by such employment.

---

money, job skills, and leads to better jobs—to disadvantaged and some deprived youth, especially in our inner cities. But these programs also serve other equally important functions. One of these, which I have touched on above, is to provide the patronage necessary for the survival of the ethnic organizations that largely administer these programs, but that also play a vital role in contemporary urban politics. Without these organizations, our big cities would be much more difficult, perhaps impossible, to govern. These new big-city "machines" are similar in function to the older big-city machines which more or less represented and served the interests of the old ethnic groups after the Civil War. These ethnic organizations give an institutional structure to ethnic communities and link them to the urban political systems.

In addition, these programs, together with other publicly supported programs, create administrative and staff jobs for the most energetic and ambitious members of the new ethnic groups—jobs and careers inside the system rather than outside and against it. In this way these public jobs are very important in the creation of new ethnic middle classes who have a stake in the existing structure of politics and in the programs of services that it provides for poor members of their own ethnic group.

Since this behavior is rewarded in much the same way that conventional skills are rewarded in other work environments, it can become habitual. These modes of behavior are, in other words, "learned." When they are antagonistic to employment in the primary sector, they must be "unlearned" if the worker is to transfer successfully out of the secondary market. Thus, for example, the very fact that so many secondary jobs accept lateness or absenteeism and adapt to it tends to encourage unstable, erratic job attachment among workers. Similarly, some secondary employers anticipate that their employees will steal. Rather than attempting to prevent it, employers accept the fact that it occurs, turn their backs, and adjust wages downward accordingly. Where supervision is harsh or abusive, and there is no institutionalized process for resolving grievances, employees often relate to their supervisors in a manner that in primary jobs would be considered insubordinate.

Or, again, employers expecting workers to be unskilled purchase either very durable or cheap, second-hand machinery and accept the careless treatment it receives. As a result, the workers who use it become accustomed to treating machinery in this way and can neither understand nor accept the greater respect accorded tools and equipment in primary employments.

To some extent, all workers in the secondary sector "learn" behavior traits on the job. In this sense, the "disadvantaged" involuntarily confined to such work may not be very different from the student, the working mother, or the moonlighter in the same job. However, the advantaged secondary workers tend to come from environments which foster different behavioral traits and, because of this, weaken the habits which develop at work. For a great many disadvantaged workers, on the other hand, the habits

which are developed at the workplace also exist in the
home and social environments as well.

It may well be that the central problem of youth in other
advanced industrial societies (at least as seen by their governments) is their transition from school to the primary labor market. From this perspective, everything depends on the quality of
their first jobs, and this would account for the enormous efforts
that these governments make to ensure that young people will
be adequately trained and counseled for regular, secure jobs
with a future and also to ensure that jobs in the primary sector
will in fact be waiting for young workers as they come into the
market. By contrast, the secondary labor market may play such
an important role in the United States for all youth that the
crucial problem here is not transition from school to the labor
market, but rather from the secondary to the primary labor
market. If that is the case, then we need to analyze more closely
the variety of functions that the secondary labor market per-
forms for different segments of youth. And to do this we need
to look more closely at the characteristics of different jobs
within the secondary market. I have only touched on one of
them—their usefulness or harmfulness in preparing people for
better jobs in the primary market.

The quality of a job's usefulness in a young person's transition to adult roles has several components, two of which may
have special significance for the way that secondary labor market jobs serve different kinds of youth. One aspect of secondary
labor market jobs, mentioned above, is the quality of work experience itself. Some jobs do in fact teach young people good
work habits, while others, as Doeringer and Piore note, teach
students to abuse machinery and reward slack discipline with
poor wages and arbitrary insensitive supervision.

A second aspect of a secondary labor market job is whether it has links to the more secure, better–paying world of the
primary labor market. Some jobs do; for example, Harrison and
Sum (1978) quote Paul Osterman on the phenomenon of
"bridge" jobs which have most of the characteristics of secondary labor market jobs but in addition "are often connected to

the Primary Labor Market via both formal subcontracting and informal personnel director information."[14]

If we combine these two dimensions in a fourfold table (Figure 3.2), we have a way of characterizing secondary labor market jobs that begins to help us analyze their functions for different kinds of youth.

Type I jobs provide good experience and training, and also help young people move into the primary market as they begin to take on adult roles and responsibilities, and especially as they get married and have children. Much nonunion construction work offers this kind of experience, in which young people acquire a variety of skills that are useful in many other kinds of jobs as well as in the organized building trades. A traditional apprenticeship is designed precisely to be a Type I job, providing training in the skills and work habits necessary to become a journeyman, while also providing institutionalized channels for moving into regular long-term work careers. But while the formal apprenticeship is so close to the regular work career that it might well be considered part of the primary market, there are many informal apprenticeships, jobs in which young people are given an opportunity to learn a trade or craft while earning low pay and perhaps little or no fringe benefits. Insofar as they also provide links to primary market jobs, such "apprenticeships" would fall in this category of Type I jobs. The "bridge jobs" that Osterman speaks of would be included here, too.

Type II jobs are often jobs in marginal, fly-by-night firms, for example, machine shops that make toys, novelties, or souvenirs for a local market. Some kinds of casual labor are included here as well. Such jobs often put workers in touch with people doing similar work in bigger unionized firms. On the other hand, they may give young workers a poor experience in handling and caring for tools, or in other aspects of work discipline.

---

[14]"These jobs are typically found in metalworking, machine repair, and similar job-shop types of firms. They pay relatively low wages and few, if any, fringe benefits. On the other hand, they tend not to impose rigid industrial discipline on their (predominantly young) workers. And they offer significant on-the-job training through informal apprenticeships of young men to older, experienced craft and technical workers" (Harrison and Sum, 1978).

Figure 3.2. A typology of secondary labor market jobs

| | | Work Experience as Preparation for Primary Labor Market Jobs | |
		Good	*Poor*
		I	II
	Good	Informal apprenticeships "Bridge" jobs Nonunion construction	Marginal manufacturing Casual labor
Job-Provided Links to Primary Labor Market Jobs			
		III	IV
	Poor	Fast food chains	Criminal and quasicriminal activities: gambling, drugs, theft, etc.

Type III jobs may teach good work habits but are thought to be "dead-end" in the sense that they do not connect people up to better primary market jobs. Jobs in fast-food chains are predominantly staffed by 16- to 22-year-olds, who perform all the tasks from operating the grill to running the cash register. But except for a tiny minority who make a career in fast food operations, the jobs are simply a way of earning some cash through part-time work while going to school or on vacation.[15]

Type IV jobs offer neither good work experience (that is, good for future jobs and careers) nor good connections to better legitimate jobs. Many young lower class people are, at some

[15] In the San Francisco Bay Area, McDonald's has initiated a school and vocational counseling service for its young employees, apparently to provide the links to education and to the primary labor market that its own jobs do not provide. If this project is successful, jobs with such associated counseling services would be elevated to Type I. McDonald's, it appears, is trying to improve the attractiveness of its own part-time employment.

time and to some degree, part of a juvenile subculture on the periphery of the economy of crime, but the majority leaves it for the legitimate economy when better opportunities present themselves. But work in the illegal economy usually doesn't encourage movement to legal jobs, and for some youth, usually those with few or no family resources, these Type IV jobs become a trap, especially when they pay well enough to make available legitimate jobs look overdemanding and underpaid.

There may well be other characteristics of secondary market jobs, as of young people, that are worth exploring. Research along these lines will necessarily study the processes by which different kinds of youth connect with different parts of the secondary labor market as they make (or try to make) the transition to adult roles. Such research will involve a study of social and psychological processes of late adolescence and early adulthood in different class and ethnic groups. That, I believe, is a necessary supplement to an analysis based on what may be not very reliable statistics on rates of employment and unemployment in different parts of the population of youth.[16] A preoccupation with those numbers can distract us from a study of the underlying processes by which youth do (or do not) make the transition to responsible and productive adult roles. And it is an understanding of those processes, as they vary for different types of youth, that constitutes a major part of the knowledge base we need for the design of more effective programs for youth. Another valuable part of that knowledge base would be a better understanding of the mechanisms by which public policies and programs can affect the processes through which young people become fully adult.

Joint Effects

I suggested earlier that how youth use secondary labor market jobs is a function of characteristics both of the job and of the young people, their families, and other institutional resources available to them. For example, a young man or woman who is

[16] For discussions of sources of error in unemployment statistics, see Clarkson and Meiners (1977), Devens (1978), Shiskin and Stein (1975) and Gutmann (1979). See also the testimony by Shiskin (1978).

a church member, or part of an ethnic community, may have many people able and ready to help him or her "get started." Such networks function in two ways: They tell youngsters where job openings are, and they provide the kind of informal character reference that employers want. Many if not most "regular" jobs are filled through these informal networks of friends, relatives, neighbors, relatives of friends, and friends of relatives.

For young men or women who are part of such networks, it does not much matter what the characteristics are of any temporary secondary market job they may hold before they "settle down." For example, college students have a long history, at least in this country, of working summers at low status "dead-end" jobs without anybody worrying about the effect of those jobs on their careers. Indeed, a summer job waiting on tables or working as a laborer on a construction site is likely to be more a source of pride than of anxiety to middle class parents, who generally like the idea of their children earning money in their spare time while learning something about a part of the world of work that most of them will never experience again after leaving college.

If we look at our typologies of jobs and of youth together, we can see that school, family, friends, church, and job are *alternative* resources for helping young men and women become responsible and productive adults. The family is especially important, because it not only provides (or does not provide) resources of advice, money, job leads, and the like to its young adult members, but also shapes their characters in ways that determine whether they are able to take advantage of any of the resources available to them, whoever provides them. If a young man or woman has the psychological and emotional capacity for dealing with the world—is able to establish personal relationships, postpone gratification, accept and discharge responsibility, and the like—then he or she may use any or all of these institutional responses in moving toward adult roles. For example, an advantaged middle-class boy or girl with college-educated parents may use family ties to choose a college and even a college major, and, with the help of the college placement office, to find a job. For such a young person, it may not much matter whether the summer vacation jobs or a job held for a year while "stopping out" of school would fall in Type I, II, or III in our typology of secondary market jobs. By contrast, a young disadvantaged person from an immigrant or relatively uneducated family may have strong personal qualities, but need more to get on in the world than his or her family can give him. That help may come from counselors and teachers in high school. Such a young person may have higher ambitions and some academic ability, and be encouraged to enroll in a community college or even gain a scholarship to a four-year private institution. But if a young man or woman from such a background does not have the ambition or inclination to go into postsecondary education, there is a relatively long period between leaving high school and getting a regular full-time job in the primary market. Depending on many factors, such a young person may not have many good leads for useful secondary labor market jobs. Here is where the federal programs for youth employment come into play. They are intended to supplement the private secondary job market and create a variety of supported or subsidized secondary labor market jobs that may be useful to young people. If we look at the jobs supported under the various titles of the Neighborhood Youth Corps and CETA, we see that they have many of the characteristics of secondary labor market jobs: They are temporary and low paying; they do not carry fringe benefits; they are not unionized; nor do they encourage strong job attachments. They are, in fact, secondary labor market jobs on public funds. But they are intended to be Type I or Type III jobs—that is, to provide good and useful work experience, and to provide some links to the primary job market. On the whole, these jobs seem to be more successful in providing good work experience than in establishing links. In any event, the public programs for youth employment can be better understood as an effort to provide a certain kind of secondary labor market job for young people who are able to use them. And this helps us understand why they are much more successful in recruiting disadvantaged youth than deprived youth.

Just as publicly supported youth programs can be seen as an effort to supplement the various resources helping young people become adults, higher education can be seen in the same way. All of higher education is to some extent a preparation for adult jobs and careers. Despite much rhetoric to the contrary, there is no clear distinction between "liberal" and "vocational" education: The qualities of mind, varieties of knowledge, and ways of speaking and writing that are the products of a liberal education are prerequisites for many kinds of upper-white-collar professional and administrative jobs in our society. A liberal education is indeed the vocational training for a large class of well-paid middle class occupations. Colleges also give students a circle of teachers and friends who can help at various stages in their adult careers. So a college or university education is rather like a Type I job in the secondary labor market: It is temporary, poorly paid, but provides good training for adult work and leads and links to adult jobs and careers.

The counseling and placement services of colleges and universities are especially noteworthy here as a special kind of resource for the transition to adult roles. The more skilled the job or career that a young person is aiming for, the less likely it is that his or her network of family, friends and neighbors will be able to give advice and introductions that would be helpful to gain the desired job or career. The reason is simply that the further the student goes in college or graduate school, the less likely it is that his or her family and friends will be familiar with the part of the occupational structure for which the student has qualified. So, especially for students with more modest backgrounds, college and departmental counseling services and placement offices become increasingly useful. But children of professional people will be less likely to use those resources, since they will still be able to make connections through family and other personal networks. On the whole, the use of vocational and career counseling, whether in high school or college, is a functional substitute for the personal ties and advice that can be provided by more educated parents.

But when we speak of the problems of youth, we tend to focus on the problems of young people who do not come from such advantaged backgrounds, and for whom the alternative is not a college-educated parent or the sophisticated counseling and placement services of colleges and graduate schools. We think of the much greater difficulties of young people from more modest backgrounds or from the severely disadvantaged backgrounds in which most minority youth grow up. For such youth, experience on the job is of very considerable importance in shaping their life chances. And for them, the quality and availability of good and useful secondary labor market jobs are of the greatest significance in their successful transition from youth to adult roles.

The design of effective policies for youth requires much more detailed knowledge than we now have of how different kinds of youth do or do not make the transition to adult jobs and roles. For some advantaged youth, the dice are already so heavily loaded in their favor that no further public effort is needed (beyond its very considerable support for higher education). On the other hand, the dice are so heavily loaded against some deprived youth that we can scarcely imagine any public program having an appreciable effect. But there are many young people in between who have resources of character, intelligence, motivation, and networks of family and friends, but for whom additional help—a good secondary labor market job, a glimpse of a larger world and of broader opportunities—may have effects out of all proportion to the costs and effort involved.

On the whole, we suspect that in the United States most federally supported job programs thus far have had these generally benign effects for disadvantaged youth. But the problems of deprived youth in America remain largely unsolved, perhaps not even seriously attacked outside the system of criminal justice. Until we can see these problems as different in kind and not just in degree from those that disadvantaged youth face, as problems arising not only out of financial poverty but out of a poverty of personal and social resources, we can hardly begin to address them successfully.

References

Ahmed, M. "South Asia." In *Education and Youth Employment in Less Developed Countries: Mexico and South Asia.* Berkeley, Calif.: Carnegie Council on Higher Education, 1978.

Bailey, S. K. "Education, Jobs and Community Services: What Directions for National Policies?" In Barbara Burn (Ed.), *Access, Systems, Youth and Employment.* Paper presented to the ICED–Aspen Seminar Program, Aspen, Colo.: July 30, 1976.

Barton, P. *Juvenile Delinquency, Work and Education.* Unpublished report prepared for the U.S. Department of Health, Education, and Welfare. Washington, D.C.: National Manpower Institute, 1976.

Booz, Allen, and Hamilton. *Bildungswesen im Vergleich: Beschäftigungsprobleme Jugendlicher in ausgewählten Ländern.* Report prepared for the Federal Ministry of Education and Science, Federal Republic of Germany. Bonn: Federal Ministry for Education and Science, 1975.

Bullock, P. *Aspiration vs. Opportunity: "Careers" in the Inner City.* Ann Arbor, Mich.: Institute of Labor and Industrial Relations, University of Michigan–Wayne State University, 1973.

Business Week. "The Fast Growth of the Underground Economy." March 13, 1978, pp. 71, 73–74.

Carnegie Commission on the Future of Higher Education. *College Graduates and Jobs: Adjusting to a New Labor Market Situation.* New York: McGraw-Hill, 1973.

Carnegie Council on Policy Studies in Higher Education. *Education and Youth Employment in Contemporary Societies.* A series of volumes on selected countries. Berkeley, Calif.: 1978, 1979, and forthcoming.

Clarkson, K. W., and Meiners, R. E. "Government Statistics as a Guide to Economic Policy: Food Stamps and the Spurious Increase in the Unemployment Rates." *Policy Review,* Summer 1977, pp. 27–55.

Coleman, J. S., and others. *Youth: Transition to Adulthood.* Report of the Panel on Youth of the President's Science Advisory Committee. Washington, D.C.: June 1973.

Commission of the European Communities. *Unemployment of Young People.* Unpublished tables. Brussels: 1976.

Commission of the European Communities. *Monthly Statistics on the Registered Unemployed in the Community, September 1977.* Luxembourg: Eurostat, 1977.

Congressional Budget Office. *The Teenage Unemployment Problem: What Are the Options?* Washington, D.C.: GPO, Oct. 14, 1976.

Devens, R. M. "Food Stamps and the Spurious Rise in the Unemployment Rate Re-Examined." *Policy Review,* Winter 1978, pp. 77–87.

Doeringer, P. B., and Piore, M. J. *Internal Labor Markets and Manpower Analysis.* Lexington, Mass.: Heath, 1971.

Dresch, S. P. "Dynamics of Growth and Decline." In J. D. Millett (Ed.), *Managing Turbulence and Change.* San Francisco: Jossey–Bass, 1977.

Employment and Earnings. Jan. 1979.

Erikson, E. *Childhood and Society.* (2nd ed.) New York: Norton, 1964.

Farnsworth, C. H. "Joblessness Among Youths Is Raising Worry in Europe." *New York Times,* Dec. 13, 1976.

Feldstein, M. "The Economics of the New Unemployment." *The Public Interest,* Fall 1973, *33,* 3–42.

Fortune. "Why the Underground Economy Is Booming." Oct. 9, 1978, pp. 92–95, 98.

Freeman, R. B. *The Over-Educated American.* New York: Academic Press, 1976.

Freud, D. "A Guide to Underground Economics." *Financial Times,* April 9, 1979, p. 165.

Friedlander, S. L. *Unemployment in the Urban Core: An Analysis of Thirty Cities with Policy Recommendations.* New York: Praeger, 1972.

Gavett, T., and others. *Youth Unemployment and Minimum Wages.* Washington, D.C.: U.S. Bureau of Labor Statistics, 1970.

Gillis, J. R. *Youth and History: Tradition and Change in European Age Relations, 1770–Present.* Studies in Social Discontinuity Series. New York: Academic Press, 1974.

Gordon, D. M. (Ed.). *Problems in Political Economy: An Urban Perspective.* Lexington, Mass.: Heath, 1971.

Gordon, M. S. *Retraining and Labor Market Adjustment in Western Europe.* Washington, D.C.: U.S. Office of Manpower, Automation, and Training, 1965.

Gordon, M. S. (Ed.). *Higher Education and the Labor Market.* New York: McGraw–Hill, 1974.

Gordon, R. A. *The Need to Disaggregate the Full Employment Goal.* Washington, D.C.: National Commission on Manpower Policy, 1978.

Gramlich, E. *Impact of Minimum Wages on Other Wages, Employment and Family Incomes.* Brookings Papers on Economic Activity. Washington, D.C.: The Brookings Institution, 1976.

Gray, S. H., and Bolce, L. "Not That Job, Thanks." *New York Times,* Dec. 5, 1977.

Gutmann, P. M. "The Subterranean Economy." *Financial Analyst's Journal,* Nov.–Dec. 1977, pp. 26–27.

Gutmann, P. M. "The Grand Unemployment Illusion." *Journal of the Institute for Socioeconomic Studies,* 1979, *4* (2), 20–30.

Harrison, B., and Sum, A. "Segmented Labor Market Theory and the Measurement of Employment and Unemployment." Paper for the National Commission on Employment and Unemployment Statistics, March 1978. Mimeographed.

Hecquet, I., Verniers, C., and Cerych, L. *Recent Student Flows in Higher Education*. New York: International Council for Educational Development, 1976.

Institute of Education, European Cultural Foundation. *Between School and Work*. Paris: 1976.

International Encyclopedia of the Social Sciences. Vol. 4. *Delinquency.* New York: Crowell-Collier and Macmillan, 1968.

Janne, H. *Education and Youth Employment in Belgium.* Berkeley, Calif.: Carnegie Council on Higher Education, 1979.

Kato, H. *Education and Youth Employment in Japan.* Berkeley, Calif.: Carnegie Council on Higher Education, 1978.

Kerr, C. "The Balkanization of Labor Markets." In *Labor Markets and Wage Determinants.* Berkeley: University of California Press, 1977.

Killingsworth, C. C. "Negroes in a Changing Labor Market." In A. M. Ross and H. Hill (Eds.), *Employment, Race, and Poverty.* New York: Harcourt, Brace & World, 1967.

Köditz, V. *The Netherlands: Occupational Choice and Motivation of Youth.* Heidelberg: Arbeitsgruppe für Empirische Bildungsforschung e.V., Sept. 1977a. Duplicated.

Köditz, V. *F. R. of Germany: Occupational Choice and Motivation of Youth.* Heidelberg: Arbeitsgruppe für Empirische Bildungsforschung e.V., Nov. 1977b. Duplicated.

Lasko, R. "The Work Experience Programme." *Department of Employment Gazette* (Great Britain), March 1978, pp. 294-297.

Levine, R. A., and Lyon, D. W. "Studies in Public Welfare: A Review Article." *Journal of Human Resources,* 1975, *10* (4), 544-546.

Levitan, S. A. "Job Corps Experience with Manpower Training." *Monthly Labor Review,* 1975, *98* (10), 3-11.

Lewis, F. "The Trouble with Europe." *New York Times Magazine,* April 2, 1978, p. 13.

Liberska, B. *Education and Youth Employment in Poland.* Berkeley, Calif.: Carnegie Council on Higher Education, 1979.

Liebow, E. *Tally's Corner.* Boston: Little, Brown, 1967.

Maclure, S. *Education and Youth Employment in Great Britain.* Berkeley, Calif.: Carnegie Council on Higher Education, 1979.

Medina, A. H., and Izquierdo, C. M. "Mexico." In *Education and Youth Employment in Less Developed Countries: Mexico and South Asia.* Berkeley, Calif.: Carnegie Council on Higher Education, 1978.

Moore, D. J. "Nelson and Colne College." In Institute of Education, European Cultural Foundation, *Between School and Work.* Paris: 1976.

National Committee on Employment of Youth. *The Transition from School to Work: A Study of Laws, Regulations and Practices Restricting Work Experience and Employment Opportunities for Youth.* New York: 1975.

Newsweek. "Black Youth: A Lost Generation?" Aug. 7, 1978, pp. 22, 24, 29–30, 33–34.

New York Times. "Unreported Work May Cost U.S. Billions in Taxes and Impair Plans." Jan. 15, 1978.

Organization for Economic Cooperation and Development. *Beyond Compulsory Schooling: Options and Changes in Upper Secondary Education.* Paris: 1976.

Organization for Economic Cooperation and Development. *Entry of Young People into Working Life.* Paris: 1977a.

Organization for Economic Cooperation and Development. *High Level Conference on Youth Unemployment.* Item 4. *Country Position Papers.* Paris: 1977b.

Organization for Economic Cooperation and Development. *High Level Conference on Youth Unemployment.* Item 4. *Diagnosis.* Paris: Nov. 9, 1977c. Duplicated.

Organization for Economic Cooperation and Development. *High Level Conference on Youth Unemployment.* Point 5. *Examen des mesures adoptées dans les pays membres: tableaux statistiques.* Paris: Dec. 1, 1977d.

Organization for Economic Cooperation and Development. Manpower and Social Affairs Committee. *Demographic Trends: Their Labour Market and Social Implications.* Annex 2 (tables). Paris: April 21, 1978.

Organization for Economic Cooperation and Development. *Economic Outlook.* Paris: Dec. 1978.

Organization for Economic Cooperation and Development. *Policies for Apprenticeship.* Paris: 1979.

Organization for Economic Cooperation and Development. *Labour Force Statistics: Quarterly Supplement to the Yearbook.* Paris: quarterly.

Piore, M. J. *Undocumented Workers and United States Immigration Policy.* Cambridge, Mass.: Center for International Studies, Massachusetts Institute of Technology, 1977.

Rehn, G., and Petersen, H. *Education and Youth Employment in Sweden and Denmark.* Berkeley, Calif.: Carnegie Council on Higher Education, forthcoming.

Reubens, B. *Bridges to Work: International Comparisons of Transition Services.* Montclair, N.J.: Allenheld and Osmun, 1977.

Reuterberg, S. W. "The New Swedish Gymnasium School." In Institute of Education, European Cultural Foundation, *Between School and Work.* Paris: 1976.

Robison, D. *Training and Jobs Programs in Action: Case Studies in Private-Sector Initiatives for the Hard-to-Employ.* New York: Committee for Economic Development, 1978.

Schoos, J. *Denmark: Occupational Choice and Motivation of Youth.* Heidelberg: Arbeitsgruppe für Empirische Bildungsforschung e.V., Nov. 1977. Duplicated.

Sellin, B. "The *Kollegstufe* in North Rhine-Westphalia." In Institute of Education, European Cultural Foundation, *Between School and Work.* Paris, 1976.

Shiskin, J. (Commissioner, U.S. Bureau of Labor Statistics) Testimony, Hearings of the Subcommittees on the Departments of Labor and Health, Education, and Welfare. 95th Cong., 2nd sess. (Part I, Department of Labor) Washington, D.C.: GPO, 1978.

Shiskin, J., and Stein, R. L. "Problems in Measuring Unemployment." *Monthly Labor Review*, 1975, *98* (8), 2–10.

Smith, S., and Lasko, R. "After the Work Experience Programme: Following Their Progress." *Department of Employment Gazette* (Great Britain), August 1978, pp. 901–907.

Stack, C. B. *All Our Kin*. New York: Harper & Row, 1974.

Striner, H. E. "Recurrent Education and Manpower Training in Great Britain." *Monthly Labor Review*, 1975, *98* (9), 30–34.

The President. *Employment and Training Report of the President, 1977*. Washington, D.C.: 1977.

The President. *Employment and Training Report of the President, 1978*. Washington, D.C.: 1978.

The President. *Economic Report of the President, 1979*. Washington, D.C.: 1979.

Timpane, M., and others. *Youth Policy in Transition*. Santa Monica, Calif.: The Rand Corporation, 1976.

Trow, M. "Thoughts on Youth: Transition to Adulthood." *Working Paper*. Graduate School of Public Policy, University of California, Berkeley, 1974.

Trow, M. "Reflections on Policies for Youth." *Working Paper*. Graduate School of Public Policy, University of California, Berkeley, 1976.

Trow, M. "Elite and Mass Higher Education: American Models and European Realities." In *Research into Higher Education: Processes and Structures*. Report from a conference in June 1978. Stockholm: National Board of Universities and Colleges, 1979.

United Nations Educational, Scientific, and Cultural Organization. *Statistical Yearbook, 1975*. New York: 1975. Published annually.

U.S. Bureau of the Census. "Estimates of the Population of the United States, by Single Years of Age, Color, and Sex: 1900 to 1959." *Current Population Reports*. Series P–25, no. 311. Washington, D.C.: GPO, 1965.

U.S. Bureau of the Census. "Estimates of the Population of the United States, by Age, Sex, and Race: April 1, 1960 to July 1, 1973." *Current Population Reports*. Series P–25, no. 519. Washington, D.C.: GPO, 1974.

U.S. Bureau of the Census. "Estimates of the Population of the United States, by Age, Sex, and Race: April 1, 1960 to July 1, 1973." *Current tion Reports*. Series P–25, no. 614. Washington, D.C.: GPO, 1976.

U.S. Bureau of the Census. "Estimates of the Population of the United States, by Age, Sex, and Race: July 1, 1974 to 1976." *Current Population Reports*. Series P–25, no. 643. Washington, D.C.: GPO, 1977a.

U.S. Bureau of the Census. "Projections of the Population of the United States: 1977 to 2050." *Current Population Reports*. Series P–25, no. 704. Washington, D.C.: GPO, 1977b.

U.S. Bureau of Labor Statistics. *International Comparisons of Unemployment.* Bulletin 1979. Washington, D.C.: GPO, 1978.

U.S. Manpower Administration. *Low-Income Labor Markets and Urban Manpower Programs: A Critical Assessment.* Washington, D.C.: GPO, 1972.

Vocational Foundation, Inc. *Our Turn to Listen: A White Paper on Unemployment, Education and Crime Based on Extensive Interviews with New York City Teenage Dropouts.* New York: n.d.

von Dohnanyi, K. *Education and Youth Employment in the Federal Republic of Germany.* Berkeley, Calif.: Carnegie Council on Higher Education, 1978.

Wall Street Journal. "Underground Economy." Nov. 30, 1978, pp. 1, 19.

Wheatley, D. C. "Sixth-Form Colleges: Their Present Situation." In Institute of Education, European Cultural Foundation, *Between School and Work.* Paris: 1976.

Wirtz, W., and Goldstein, H. "Measurement and Analysis of Work Training." *Monthly Labor Review,* 1975, *98* (9), 19–26.

Wool, H. "Future Labor Supply for Lower Level Occupations." *Monthly Labor Review,* 1976, *99* (3), 22–31.

Young, A. M. "Students, Graduates, and Dropouts in the Labor Market, October 1975." *Monthly Labor Review,* 1976, *99* (6), 37–41.